1   ANTICHRIST UNMASKED

ANTICHRIST UNMASKED

Antichrist

UNMASKED

**"And have no fellowship with the unfruitful
works of darkness, but rather <u>expose them</u>."
Ephesians 5:11 NKJV**

ANTICHRIST UNMASKED

QR Code Instructions

This book being about the Antichrist; the irony of using QR code technology to expose him I find amusing. I want my readers to have the option if they desire to have an interactive and more in-depth study of this person the Bible calls the Antichrist. QR codes are not the "Mark of the Beast," though they have been used for nefarious purposes in the name of Corona. With QR code technology, you, as the reader, can use your smartphone or tablet to scan codes that will, in turn, take you directly to all resources available, including a few videos. As you're reading along in the book, this will give you easy, instant access to the subjects' verifiable sources.

1) Every smartphone and tablet should have a QR code scanner; some are imbedded in the camera. Just aim camera at code and a link should appear for you to click on. If you can't find it, search in your settings. You can always download a free QR code scanner from your app store if necessary.

2) Any paragraph with highlighted words will have a corresponding QR code in the margins for you to scan with your smartphone or tablet that will take you directly to the available source.

Test

It's That Easy!

ANTICHRIST UNMASKED

Contents

ANTICHRIST UNMASKED

Introduction

I know what you're thinking; there is no way anyone could possibly know who the final Antichrist will be. One may say many have claimed several people as Antichrist in the past; for example, Nero Caesar, Antiochus Epiphanes, Putin of Russia, King Charles III, Hitler, the Pope, and every American president has been speculated as possible Antichrist, and the list goes on. You're absolutely right in that regard. Every time some strange or ominous figure arises on the world seen, one of the first speculations is that "he might be the Antichrist!" It's always an emotional response to one or two characteristics a person may have with no solid Biblical foundation at all.

In this book, we will first take a comprehensive Biblical study of this person called the Antichrist before we even start trying to connect any dots to anyone presently. The Bible gives us a mountain of evidence about this person called the Antichrist. Suppose you first know what the Bible says about the Antichrist and not just a few personal characteristics. In that case, you will be Biblically prepared to recognize him even before he is revealed globally. Now I say that boldly because the Bible does give us so much information about this person called the Antichrist. The information was given to us for one purpose; so that "only" those living in the last days could recognize him and not be deceived but rather expose him for who he really is; the "man of sin." When Antichrist is revealed, global spiritual warfare will be at a level never seen before in history or ever will be seen again in the future. The mandate for the Church during this time will be to continue the

Great Commission leading those away from Antichrist and to the one and only truth; Jesus Christ. As I've mentioned in my previous books, the Church needs to be mentally, emotionally, physically, and, most importantly, spiritually prepared for the war we are about to encounter. Sadly, for the most part, the Church is not being prepared by its leaders presently for this particular final battle.

One of the highlights of this book is that I believe I'm going to show you something in the Bible for the "first time" that no one has realized points precisely to one undeniable individual. There is one Bible prophecy with many moving parts that points directly to a person as the Antichrist. In this book, as we thoroughly unmask the Antichrist, we will walk together through this unbelievable passage in the Bible. You will be stunned and amazed at the pinpoint accuracy of the individual the Bible points to.

I encourage you to please don't skip around in this book. Know your enemy and Be Ready! Get your Bible out and your phone if you desire while you follow along as we genuinely, for the first time, scripturally unmask the Antichrist.

The Four Beast

As we begin this unmasking of the Antichrist and dive deeper, as a refresher, we are going to go over some things I've written in my first book, "The EndTime is Now." We will be digging deeper with some fresh insights, and whether you have read my previous books or not, this book will provide a comprehensive Biblical study of this person called the Antichrist. Later as we continue to unmask this man of sin, you will see how all the Biblical dots point to only one person right now. Let's begin the unmasking.

No one will completely understand the prophecies until the time of the end.

8Although I heard, I did not understand. Then I said, "My lord, what shall be the end of these things?"
9And he said, "Go your way, Daniel, for the words are closed up and sealed till the time of the end.
Daniel 12:8-9 NKJV

THE 4 BEAST

1In the first year of Belshazzar king of Babylon, Daniel had a dream and visions of his head while on his bed. Then he wrote down the dream, telling the main facts. 2 Daniel spoke, saying, "I saw in my vision by night, and behold, the four winds of heaven were stirring up the Great Sea. 3And four great beasts came up from the sea, each different from the other. Daniel 7:1-3 NKJV

Many scholars have taught that the four beasts, the lion is Babylon, the Bear is Media Persia, Leopard is Greece, ten horn kingdom is Rome.

This has traditionally been a commonly excepted explanation of this prophecy. However, *(Daniel 8:20-21)* says the ram is Media and Persia, and the goat is Greece.

20The ram which you saw, having the two horns—they are the kings of Media and Persia. 21And the male goat is the kingdom of Greece..... Daniel 8:20-21 NKJV

The kingdom of Babylon and Media Persia doesn't exist any longer. Daniel chapter 7 says all these kingdoms will be here during the time of the 2nd coming of Jesus.

Another proof that the four beasts that Daniel is referring to they must arise after Christ's birth; is found in *(Revelation chapters 12-14)*. This single account starts with Jesus' birth and concludes at his 2nd coming. Jesus was born after ancient Babylon, ancient Media & Persia, and ancient Greece. The Lion, Bear, and Leopard are kingdoms that arise after Jesus' birth but before his 2nd coming. Seminaries try to teach that Daniel chapter 7 mirrors Daniel chapter 2, Nebuchadnezzar's dream. This is totally off base, and if you believe this, you will be way off on your foundational understanding of end times and the book of Revelation. I will cover this more in the section "The Antichrist."

We don't have to guess what the four beasts represent. Daniel 7:17, 23 makes it clear that they represent kingdoms or nations and the rulers of these nations.

17'Those great beasts, which are four, are four kings which arise out of the earth....

23"Thus he said:
'The fourth beast shall be
A fourth kingdom on earth,
Which shall be different from all other kingdoms,
And shall devour the whole earth,
Trample it and break it in pieces. Daniel 7:17, 23 NKJV

ANTICHRIST UNMASKED

We also know that these four beasts are the kingdoms represented during the time of the end of human government to the transition to the kingdom of God. Therefore, if these beasts are represented today, we know we are the generation of the time of the end.

9"I watched till the thrones were put in place,
And the Ancient of Days was seated;......Daniel 7:9 NKJV

The Ancient of Days refers to Jesus. This is the human government transitioned to Godly.

Daniel 7:11 is about the Antichrist.

11"I watched then because of the sound of the pompous words which the horn was speaking; I watched till the beast was slain, and its body destroyed and given to the burning flame. Daniel 7:11 NKJV

This passage also parallels *(Revelation 19:20)*.

20Then the beast was captured, and with him the false prophet who worked signs in his presence, by which he deceived those who received the mark of the beast and those who worshiped his image. These two were cast alive into the lake of fire burning with brimstone.
Revelation 19:20 NKJ

*12As for the **rest of the beasts,** they had their dominion taken away, yet their lives were prolonged for a season and a time. Daniel 7:12 NKJV*

Rest of the beast (nations). They had their dominion (power) taken away. They will be allowed to live into the millennium. This tells us Jesus will return during the time of these nations (Beast). So who are these 4 Beast? God picked symbols that have meaning during the endtime.

4The first was like a lion, and had eagle's wings. I watched till its wings were plucked off; and it was lifted up from the earth and made to stand on two feet like a man, and a man's heart was given to it. Daniel 7:4 NKJV

LION - is the official symbol of Great Britain.

Verse 4 also states eagle's wings were growing out of the lion until Daniel watched the wings plucked off.

EAGLES WINGS- is the Official animal symbol of the United States; furthermore, the United States came from Great Britain *(wings plucked off).*
"made to stand on two feet like a man, and a man's heart was
given to it." This can be interpreted as the birth of a nation. Interestingly enough, the United States also has another iconic symbol, Uncle Sam.

Daniel, over 2500 years ago, saw the breaking of the U.S. from Great Britain. The Declaration of Independence!

Another interesting personal observation is that our Independence was declared on 7-4-1776, and this passage is found in Daniel 7:4. This observation doesn't necessarily mean anything, but it is interesting.

In *(Daniel 7:5)* we find the Bear.

5"And suddenly another beast, a second, like a bear. It was raised up on one side, and had three ribs in its mouth between its teeth. And they said thus to it: 'Arise, devour much flesh!' Daniel 7:5 NKJV

BEAR - is Russia's iconic symbol.

"After this I looked, and there was another, like a leopard, which had on its back four wings of a fowl. The beast also had four heads, and dominion was given to it."
Daniel 7:6 NKJV

4 HEADED LEOPARD with FOWL WINGS

Several factors come into play when determining the 3rd beast. Germany's animal symbol is a black eagle; however, the eagle symbol has  already been used in these prophetic passages to describe most certainly the United States. Germany does have a prominent symbol that represents the leopard. Germany's Leopard tanks have been used primarily in European armies since the 1960s.

Germany has always been at the center of European history. The four heads are the number of times a nation will rise and fall. It also states in *(Daniel 7:6)* that it has the wings of a fowl. Therefore another kingdom is associated with it.

The four heads are the 4 Reichs.

1. Holy Roman Empire of (962-1806)
2. The German Empire (1871-1918) end of WW1
3. Adolf Hitlers Rule (1933-1945) ended at WW2
4. It seems to be rising today through the European Union, controlled by Germany & France.

The Wings of the Fowl- This nation's official emblem belongs to France, the Rooster.

France and Germany- alliance (Franco-German Alliance), ever since WW2, they have been working together in which today has led to the European Union.

7"After this I saw in the night visions, and behold, a fourth beast, dreadful and terrible, exceedingly strong. It had huge iron teeth; it was devouring, breaking in pieces, and trampling the residue with its feet. It was different from all the beasts that were before it, and it had ten horns. Daniel 7:7 NKJV

The 4th beast is a 10 HORN BEAST

We know from *(Daniel 7:24)* that the 10 horns represent 10 kings (an alliance of 10 nations) that shall rule with the Antichrist.

24The ten horns are ten kings
Who shall arise from this kingdom.
And another shall rise after them;
He shall be different from the first ones,And shall subdue three kings. Daniel 7:24 NKJV

23"Thus he said:
'The fourth beast shall be
A fourth kingdom on earth,
Which shall be different from all other kingdoms,
And shall devour the whole earth,
Trample it and break it in pieces. Daniel 7:23 NKJV

The 4th beast is a picture of a one-world government system. We are watching this system develop today.

So what will be the role of the United States during the endtime?

If we look at *(Revelation chapter 13)*, we find the four beasts of *(Daniel chapter 7)* mentioned again as a cohesive unit or combo beast. Not in Daniel chapter 2 as seminaries try to teach.

*1Then I stood on the sand of the sea. And I saw a beast rising up out of the sea, having seven heads and **ten horns**, and on his horns ten crowns, and on his heads a blasphemous name. 2Now the beast which I saw was like a **leopard**, his feet were like the feet of a **bear**, and his mouth like the mouth of a **lion**.....Revelation 13:1-3 NKJV*

This is the one-world government led by the Antichrist. One thing you don't find anywhere in Revelation, chapter 13, is the eagles' wings. So, where are the eagle's wings? Well, if you back up to the previous chapter, Revelations chapter 12 shows us where the eagle's wings are.

*14But the woman was given two **wings of a great eagle**, that she might fly into the wilderness to her place, where she is nourished for a **time and times and half a time**, from the presence of the serpent. Revelation 12:14 NKJV*

The United States will be right by Israel's (the woman) side in opposition to the Antichrist and his one-world government all during the 3 1/2 year great tribulation. You may be thinking to yourself, but the Bible says all nations will be coming against Jerusalem, found in *(Zechariah 14:2)*. My answer to that is, could it be that what is referenced here is the "United Nations" as "all nations"? After all, who makes the decisions on behalf of all nations now? The "United Nations" can certainly be interpreted as being "all nations." The United States defending Israel will not be the popular stance in the eyes of the world during the endtime, but it's always better to stand with God than Satan *(Genesis 12:3)*. The

ANTICHRIST UNMASKED

U.S. has been more supportive of Israel than any other nation throughout history. Also, I would like to add that the United Nations has passed more sanctions against Israel than any other nation on the planet, bar none. The United States has vetoed just about all of them to defend Israel.

Regardless of present or future administrations and the direction they may take the United States on policies, the Bible prophecies always come to pass. The United States (Eagles Wings) will defend Israel throughout the entire 3 1/2 year tribulation that authority is granted to the Antichrist. You probably say, "I thought the great tribulation was seven years?." There is a final seven-year period; however, the Antichrist is only granted authority to rule for 3 1/2 years of it. He will rise to power without control in the first half of the seven years. We will cover this more in-depth later.

*5And he was given a mouth speaking great things and blasphemies, and he was given authority to continue for **forty-two months**. (3 1/2 years) Revelation 13:5 NKJV*

In conclusion, having a correct understanding of Daniel's four beasts is very important in understanding other Bible prophecies. This is a must-know Principle.

33And they that understand among the people shall instruct many...Daniel 11:33 NKJV

Antichrist

I n this chapter, we will discover a lot about the Antichrist as we continue to unmask him. For example, what part of the world will he come from? Is he the white horse of the apocalypse mentioned in Revelation 6:2, the first Seal? Who is his partner, the false prophet, and can we unmask the false prophet? What are the qualifications and Biblical characteristics of the Antichrist? Will the Antichrist have any opposition? If so, who will it be? If the Antichrist is the one who confirms the covenant of Daniel 9:27 that begins the final seven years, why is he only granted authority for 3 1/2 years? Will the Church be around to see the Antichrist? We will answer all these questions and much more, so let's begin.

The Holy Roman Empire has always been ruled by a political leader and a spiritual leader. The Bible prophecies that the Holy Roman Empire will be ruled again by a political leader and spiritual leader. The political leader will be the Antichrist, and the spiritual leader will be the False Prophet. Satan himself will be the one giving these two their power and, by doing so, forming the unholy trinity (Satan, Antichrist, False Prophet). Let's look at the Bible to see what's revealed about the Antichrist.

John identifies a specific person as the Antichrist while also teaching that there are many other Antichrists.

ANTICHRIST UNMASKED

18Little children, it is the last hour; and as you have heard that the Antichrist is coming, even now many antichrists have come, by which we know that it is the last hour.
1 John 2:18 NKJV

Names given to the Antichrist:

2 Thessalonians 2:3-4 "Man of Sin" and "Son of Perdition"
2 Thessalonians 2:8   "that wicked"
Daniel 7:8   the "little horn"
1John 2:18   Antichrist
Revelation 13:4-5   the "Beast"

Antichrist - One who denies or opposes Christ. One who puts himself in the place of Christ.

Notice from the list above that I did not mention the white horse of the apocalypse that most also assume is the Antichrist. Most Bible scholars believe the final seven years begin with the first Seal, the white horse they call the Antichrist. The reason they think this is because they have a misunderstanding of the chronology of the book of Revelation. The book of Revelation is not in chronological order. A lot of confusion comes into play for most when trying to understand the book of Revelation. One reason is that they try to compare the Seals, Trumpets, and Bowls as all events confined within a seven-year timeline.

The misconception is that they believe these three groups of seven all take place during the tribulation period and are, at times, referring to the same events during the tribulation. This is why scholars are confused, and contradictions are made when interpreting these three groups, which leads to a domino effect of misinterpreting everything else in the book of Revelation. John wasn't writing about events that were only to take place during the final seven years; however, he was writing about future events that

ANTICHRIST UNMASKED

were to take place beyond John's present time until the Rapture of the Church and Christ's 2nd coming. Nowhere in Revelation does it state that the events spoken of by John are limited to the final seven years only. Some of these events will happen during the last seven years; however, that doesn't mean some haven't already occurred. If you're only looking for these events to take place during the final seven years, you will be lost. The first Seal found in Revelation chapter 6 doesn't begin the final seven years. Daniel 9:27, the confirmation of the covenant, is what starts the final seven-year period.

I will not be covering the seven seals, trumpets, and bowls in this book. I've covered that topic in great detail in my first book, "The EndTime Is Now," however, for clarity, I will bring to light Biblically what the white horse of the first Seal is.

The term "Seal" is derived from the tradition of placing a seal on specified files or documents that prevents anyone from reviewing the files without receiving a court order from a judge. Here in Revelation is not the first time the term Seal has been used; remember, Daniel was told in (Daniel 12) that the words he wrote would be sealed until the time of the end, and only the wise would understand. Also, God told John in Revelation chapter 10 to Seal up the things which the seven thunders uttered and not to write them. Here in Revelation, Jesus is simply revealing information to us that would only be understood during the time of the end for our benefit. This first Seal is not the beginning of Jesus' final wrath. Because these are Seals, Jesus, as the Judge, is the only one who can open the seals. This is why the Lamb of God is mentioned in every Seal that is opened. You can read about this further in chapter 5 of Revelation.

ANTICHRIST UNMASKED

God's wrath comes when the seven Bowls are administered. These Bowls will be a targeted campaign against the Antichrist, False Prophet, and all that follow after the Antichrist. We, as Christians, will not suffer God's wrath. In the next chapter, we will discuss the timing of God's wrath of the seven bowls. So, what or who is this white horse of the first Seal?

The WHITE HORSE *(Revelation 6:2)*

2And I saw, and behold a white horse: and he that sat on him had a bow; and a crown was given unto him: and he went forth conquering, and to conquer. Revelation 6:2

He had a bow with no arrows; however, he went out conquering. Communism, Capitalism, and Catholicism are all powers that are always reaching for power and have been at the center of wars throughout history. The Roman Catholic Church began around 590 AD.

The Pope wears white because it represents holiness, and he has always been called your holiness. The Pope's helicopter is white, his car is white, and his airplane is white. I'm sure if he had a horse, it would probably be white too? White is the official color of Catholicism. The power hub of the Pope is concentrated in Vatican City inside Rome, Italy, and is considered a theocracy. The "Holy See" is the name given to the government of the Roman Catholic Church, which is led by the Pope as the bishop of Rome. As such, the Holy See's authority extends over Catholics throughout the world. Since 1929 it has resided in Vatican City, which was established as an independent state to enable the Pope to exercise his universal authority. This also explains the bow with no arrows. On the other hand, the Antichrist will use much military force, as mentioned throughout scripture; Daniel 11:31 states, "arms shall stand on his part." This white horse is not the Antichrist.

"A crown was given unto him," originally Popes didn't wear crowns until around the 8th century, and from then own Popes have at times worn crowns. Most noted now is the triple crown that took form in the 14th century. Very interesting how dots start connecting. The 1st Seal, the White Horse, is Catholicism.

If you're interested in learning more about the Seals, Trumpets, and Bowls, please read my first book's study on these three groups. As a teaser, I will say at the time of the writing of this book, the first four Seals are already opened, and the first five Trumpets have blown. Presently we are just before the 5th Seal and 6th Trumpet, while all of the Bowls of wrath have yet to be unleashed. So yes, we are well off into the end times with the final seven years at the doorstep.

Where will the Antichrist come from?

8I was considering the horns, and there was another horn, a little one, coming up among them, before whom three of the first horns were plucked out by the roots. And there, in this horn, were eyes like the eyes of a man, and a mouth speaking pompous words. Daniel 7:8 NKJV

The Antichrist will arise out of a ten-kingdom alliance. We know from the previous chapter that these horns represent kings or kingdoms. We know that these ten kings are the same ten kings represented by Daniel chapter 2 of the ten toes, representing the last of the five kingdoms on earth that would rule the world from about 600BC - 2nd coming of Jesus. Here is a list of the last five kingdoms found in *(Daniel 2:32-33)*.

32This image's head was of fine gold, its chest and arms of silver, its belly and thighs of bronze, 33its legs of iron, its feet partly of iron and partly of clay. Daniel 2:32-33 NKJV

The kingdom of the head of gold was the Babylonian kingdom; it no longer exists. The chest and arms of silver were the kingdoms of the Medes and Persians; it no longer exists. The belly and thighs of bronze were the Grecian empires; it no longer exists. The legs of iron were the old Roman Empire (197BC-284AD), and it no longer exists. *Daniel 2:33* describes later another kingdom whose iron mingles with clay to make the feet; this is the 5th and final kingdom that is rising today, the reborn Holy Roman Empire.

*42And as the **toes of the feet were partly of iron and partly of clay,** so the kingdom shall be partly strong and partly fragile. 43As you saw iron mixed with ceramic clay, they will mingle with the seed of men; but they will not adhere to one another, just as iron does not mix with clay. 44And <u>in the days of these kings</u> the God of heaven will set up a kingdom which shall never be destroyed; and the kingdom shall not be left to other people; it shall break in pieces and consume all these kingdoms, and it shall stand forever. Daniel 2:42-44 NKJV*

The Holy Roman Empire has always been from Europe. This is describing during the endtime, the 5th kingdom with feet of iron combined with a new element, " Clay," which symbolizes the reborn Holy Roman Empire. Pay attention to see that the ten toes are iron mingled with Clay; this means the ten horn Kingdom of *Daniel 7:8* will come from Europe, the Holy Roman Empire. This reborn Holy Roman Empire will consist of 2 leaders; the political leader Antichrist and the spiritual leader False Prophet. The Ruler of the Holy Roman Empire, in every instance in history's past, has always come from Europe. The Antichrist will come from Europe as its leader in the future.

The Holy Roman Empire was revived when the European Union was established and has continued to make steady strides as a cohesion since the 2009 Treaty of Lisbon. Remember, the Pope and Vatican City reside inside the parameters of Rome, Italy, as a theocracy with strong ties today with the European Union. In the end, Jesus destroys this system to set up his Kingdom that lasts forever, referenced in Vs. 44. Also, let me emphasize that Vs. 44 also says that this happens in the days of these kings (Iron mingled with clay), not past kingdoms that no longer exist. This is another depiction of the transition of human government to a Godly government ruled by Jesus that happens at his 2nd coming.

Finally, a last thought on this topic; Seminaries teach that Daniel chapter 7 with the four Beast is a mirror image of Daniel chapter 2. This is wrong, and you will be all messed up when trying to understand Bible prophecy concerning the enditimes. Daniel chapter 7 mirrors Revelation chapter 13, and instead of the kingdoms being described individually in nature like in Daniel chapter 7, they become a cohesive unit in Revelation chapter 13.

The Antichrist kingdom can be found in Revelation chapter 13.

Verses 1-8 refers to himself and his world government.

*1Then I stood on the sand of the sea. And I saw a beast rising up out of the sea, having seven heads and **ten horns**, and on his horns **ten crowns**, and on his heads a blasphemous name. 2Now the beast which I saw was like a **leopard,** his feet were like the feet of a **bear**, and his mouth like the mouth of a **lion**. The dragon gave him his power, his throne, and great authority. 3And I saw one of his heads as if it had been mortally wounded, and his deadly wound was healed. And all the world marveled and followed the beast. 4So they worshiped the dragon who gave authority to the beast; and they worshiped the beast, saying, "Who is like the beast? Who is able to make war with him?" 5And he was given a mouth speaking great things and blasphemies, and he was given authority to continue for forty-two months. 6Then he opened his mouth in blasphemy against God, to blaspheme His name, His tabernacle, and those who dwell in heaven. 7It was granted to him to make war with the Saints and to overcome them. And authority was given him over every tribe, tongue, and nation. 8All who dwell on the earth will*

ANTICHRIST UNMASKED

worship him, whose names have not been written in the Book of Life of the Lamb slain from the foundation of the world. Revelation 13:1-8 NKJV

The beast referred to here is about a kingdom and its leader. This beast described here describes the beast of *Daniel chapter 7* as now a cohesive combo beast, which will also include most of the nations on earth today known as the United Nations. This coming together of nations represents the soon-to-be one-world government led by the Antichrist himself. The nations represented here are the Leopard (Germany), the Bear (Russia), the Lion (Great Britain), and the ten-nation alliance (Holy Roman Empire). The Bible states in many passages that the Antichrist will rule this one-world system for 3 1/2 years. For Example:

25He shall speak pompous words against the Most High,
Shall persecute the Saints of the Most High,
And shall intend to change times and law.
Then the Saints shall be given into his hand
For a time and times and half a time*. Daniel 7:25 NKJV*

*5And he was given a mouth speaking great things and blasphemies, and **he was given authority to continue for forty-two months***. *Revelation 13:5 NKJV*

The Antichrist's Partner The "False Prophet"

11Then I saw another beast coming up out of the earth, and he had two horns like a lamb and spoke like a dragon. 12And he exercises all the authority of the first beast in his presence, and causes the earth and those who dwell in it to worship the first beast, whose deadly wound was healed. 13He performs great signs, so that he even makes fire come down from heaven on the earth in the sight of men.

14And he deceives those who dwell on the earth by those signs which he was granted to do in the sight of the beast, telling those who dwell on the earth to make an image to the beast who was wounded by the sword and lived. 15He was granted power to give breath to the image of the beast, that the image of the beast should both speak and cause as many as would not worship the image of the beast to be killed. Revelation 13:11-15 NKJV

The False Prophet Will be the most famous and well-respected man on the planet. He will not call the Antichrist by the name Antichrist or any other title the Bible describes the Antichrist as. Instead, the False Prophet will exalt the Antichrist and pursued people to follow after him. Let's unmask this person called the False Prophet.

(Revelation 13:11)
He will look like a lamb and speak like a dragon. He will look like a holy man, but his words come from Satan himself.

(Revelation 13:12-13)
The False Prophet will be a very powerful person. He will be able to perform miracles used in a way to deceive people, one of which makes such an impact on people that the Bible list it specifically; *"he makes fire come down from heaven."* Just because a person can perform miracles doesn't mean he is a man of God. For example, remember in *(Exodus 7:10-11)* when Moses threw down his staff, and it became a snake. Pharaoh's sorcerers did the same thing. God indeed performs miracles, and Satan is aware of this as well; this is why he will have both the False Prophet and Antichrist performing deceitful wonders to draw people unto himself.
The False Prophet will also be the head Malefactor of the Great Tribulation.

15He was granted power to give breath to the image of the beast, that the image of the beast should both speak and cause as many as would not worship the image of the beast to be killed. Revelation 13:15 NKJV

You may ask, where does it specifically state this person's title as the "False Prophet?" Revelation 19:20 perfectly parallels the description given here in chapter 13; it's here that we are given the Antichrist partner's title.

*20Then the beast was captured, and with him the **false prophet** who worked signs in his presence, by which he deceived those who received the mark of the beast and those who worshiped his image. These two were cast alive into the lake of fire burning with brimstone.*
Revelation 19:20 NKJV

As I mentioned at the beginning of this chapter, the Holy Roman Empire has always had two leaders; a political leader from Europe and a spiritual leader from Rome. This all started in 800AD when Pope LeoIII placed a crown on the head of Charlemagne, "Charles the Great," from Germany, pronouncing him emperor of the Holy Roman Empire. The Pope has always been the spiritual leader of the Holy Roman Empire.

Whoever is the Pope when the Antichrist is unveiled will be the False Prophet. I know this proclamation may sound offensive to some; however, many Catholics believe an evil pope is coming someday as well. They got this idea from St. Malachy of the 11th century, an archbishop who claimed he saw a vision of 112 popes from his time until the last Pope. The last Pope was to be an evil pope, and during the last Pope's reign, the city of Rome would be destroyed by an earthquake. This is all written in a book called "The Prophecies of St. Malachy."

I'm not espousing any of these teachings of St. Malachy at all; I'm just simply showing you why some Catholics believe that an evil pope is coming. A lot of secular scholars consider St. Malachy's visions a complete fraud. We, as Christians, know that the only true prophets are only those of the Bible. We also know that the Bible is the only source to get the truth about endtime prophecy, not false teachers, not the sun, moon, and stars, but only the word of God can guide us through the foretold events of the future. Through the fulfillment of God's prophetic word, I hope it will strengthen your faith as we see events continue to unfold. This is one of my primary intentions in writing my books, along with helping connect the dots for leaders of the faith so that they can provide real Biblical answers for the Church. That the Church may be well equipped for what lies ahead and for the greatest revival, this world has ever seen.

Interestingly though, the Bible does teach that Rome will be destroyed. The Bible calls this city "Mystery Babylon," the city of seven hills, and Rome is known as the city of seven hills. Ok, it looks like I'm going to have to explain this one, so let's look and see who "Mystery Babylon" is in Revelation.

8And another angel followed, saying, "Babylon is fallen, is fallen, that great city, because she has made all nations drink of the wine of the wrath of her fornication."
Revelation 14:8 KJV

When does the city of Mystery Babylon fall? This happens at the 7th Bowl. *(Revelation 16:19)*

19And the great city was divided into three parts, and the cities of the nations fell: and great Babylon came in remembrance before God, to give unto her the cup of the wine of the fierceness of his wrath. Revelation 16:19 KJV

This is not to be confused with Jeremiah's prophecy of Babylon found in *(Jeremiah 50:1-40)*. Furthermore, in *(Jeremiah 50:39-40)* the Bible states this land would never be inhabited again, contrary to what some are teaching that this city would have to be somehow revived to fit Revelation's prophecies of Mystery Babylon. Nimrod built the original city of Babylon shortly after the flood. This city was built over 50 miles south of today's Bagdad on the Euphrates River in Iraq. Jeremiah's prophecy of Babylon's destruction was fulfilled and hasn't been inhabited to this day. *"let God be true and every man a liar" (Romans 3:4)*. Babylon described in Revelation is called Mystery Babylon found in *(Revelation 17:1-5)*

1And there came one of the seven angels which had the seven vials, and talked with me, saying unto me, Come hither; I will shew unto thee the judgment of the great whore that sitteth upon many waters:
2With whom the kings of the earth have committed fornication, and the inhabitants of the earth have been made drunk with the wine of her fornication. 3So he carried me away in the spirit into the wilderness: and I saw a woman sit upon a scarlet coloured beast, full of names of blasphemy, having seven heads and ten horns.
4And the woman was arrayed in purple and scarlet colour, and decked with gold and precious stones and pearls, having a golden cup in her hand full of abominations and filthiness of her fornication:
5And upon her forehead was a name written, MYSTERY, BABYLON THE GREAT, THE MOTHER OF HARLOTS AND ABOMINATIONS OF THE EARTH.
Revelation 17:1-5 KJV

This "Mystery Babylon" is a different Babylon than what was spoken of by Jeremiah.

Here in Revelation chapter 17, there are a few clues to the identity of Mystery Babylon.

o 1) Notice that "Mystery Babylon" is referred to as a woman. If we go down to *verse 18*, we find that this woman is described as a great city, not a nation.

18And the woman which thou sawest is that great city, which reigneth over the kings of the earth. Revelation 17:18 KJV

o 2) In *verse 1*, we find that this woman sits on many waters. *Verse 15* explains the meaning of these many waters.

15And he saith unto me, The waters which thou sawest, where the whore sitteth, are peoples, and multitudes, and nations, and tongues. Revelation 17:15 KJV

So from the first two clues, we find that this woman is a city that's evidently the power hub that presides over a vast international system of nations. Sounds a lot like the White Horse of Revelation 6:2.

o 3) In *verse 3*, we find that this woman rides on a beast with 7 heads. *Verse 9* tells us who these 7 heads are.

9And here is the mind which hath wisdom. The seven heads are seven mountains, on which the woman sitteth. Revelation 17:9 KJV

Ok, we now know that this city sits on seven mountains. Rome is the city today that is well known as the "City of Seven Hills." Also, the Vatican claims to rule over 1.34 Billion people worldwide as of 2018 and continues to grow; we get this information from the census of the 2020

"Pontifical Yearbook." This makes the city of Rome an International power over "peoples, multitudes, nations, and tongues." For those that tried to apply this prophecy to the United States, sorry.

o 4) The woman is clothed in Purple and Scarlet *(Revelation 17:4)*. The Catholic Church's two ruling bodies are the College of Cardinals and the College of Bishops & Archbishops. The Cardinals wear red, and the Bishops wear purple. Also, I would like to add that the woman here in *Revelation, chapter 17*, is also referred to as a whore. In scripture, God uses a woman as a symbol for the Church. For instance, Christ calls the Church, his Bride. *(2 Corinthians 11:2)* refers to the true Church as a "chaste virgin to Christ." The use of a harlot by God was to describe a false Church of idolatry etc.... Just like what is being described here throughout Revelation *chapters 17-19.*

The bottom line, the Roman Catholic Church, more specifically the Vatican itself, is who the "Mystery Babylon" is. It will be this religious system that has deceived the people of the world and will continue to do so until the Battle of Armageddon. This is the religious system and its city of residence that will be utterly destroyed by Jesus at Armageddon.

Whoever the Pope is during the onset of Daniel's 70th week (final seven years) will be the "False Prophet." The Pope will point people to the Antichrist as he rises to power in the first 3 1/2 years until he is revealed globally at the mid-point. The False Prophet will be leading a one-world religious system that will eventually demand worship to the Antichrist.

The Antichrist is on the earth right now.

Some speculate that the Antichrist is a system and not a man. This can not be true. Let's look at what the Bible says.

24The ten horns are ten kings
Who shall arise from this kingdom.
And another shall rise after them;
He *shall be different from the first ones,*
And shall subdue three kings.
*25**He** shall speak pompous words against the Most High,*
Shall persecute the Saints of the Most High,
And shall intend to change times and law.
*Then the Saints shall be given into **his** hand*
For a time and times and half a time. Daniel 7:24-25

This passage references the Antichrist as a male figure, "He," not "It," and it also refers to the Antichrist as a king, so he would have to be a human male ruler.

*3Let no one deceive you by any means; for that Day will not come unless the falling away comes first, and the **man of sin** is revealed, the son of perdition, 4who opposes and exalts **himself** above all that is called God or that is worshiped, so that **he** sits as God in the temple of God, showing **himself** that **he** is God. 2nd Thessalonians 2:3-4*

This passage states this will be a man that sits in the Temple, claiming to be God. This is also the description of the Abomination of Desolation described by Daniel and Jesus in Matthew chapter 24.

Though the Antichrist will have a global system that's actually in the last stage of development right now, I hope no one is confused about whether the Antichrist is an actual person? These few scriptures of many, along with the long list of attributes provided later, should clear up any doubts.

The Antichrist will confirm a covenant
mentioned in *Daniel 9:27*.

*27Then he shall **confirm a covenant** with many for one week;*
But in the middle of the week
He shall bring an end to sacrifice and offering.
And on the wing of abominations shall be one who makes desolate,
Even until the consummation, which is determined,
Is poured out on the desolate." Daniel 9:27 NKJV

This covenant that is being referred to here is found in *Genesis 15:18*.

*18On the same day the **Lord made a covenant with Abram**, saying: "To your descendants I have given this land, from the river of Egypt to the great river, the River Euphrates Genesis 15:18 NKJV*

Here God made a covenant with Abraham stating that this land would be his and his descendants forever. The covenant the Antichrist confirms will, in essence, agree on Israel's right to exist. The word "confirm" means to make it better or stronger, so something else would have to exist to strengthen it.

On August 13th, 2020, the United Arab of Emirates signed an exclusive peace deal with Israel. This was the official launch of what is now known as the "Abraham Accords." Interesting name given to it, don't you say? United Arab of Emirates was the first country to sign onto the Abraham Accords and the third country to make peace with Israel since they were declared a nation in 1948. Since August 2020, Morocco and Sudan have joined the agreement totaling five nations at the time of the writing of this book who have made peace with Israel. Many more are said to join in the very near future.

ANTICHRIST UNMASKED

When the UAE first joined the 'Abraham Accords,' the Palestinian Leadership reaction to it was, to be expected, not good. They tweeted, *"Please don't do us a favor. We are nobody's fig leaf!"* I found this comment very revealing and prophetic; keep in mind they do not read the Bible.

*32"Now learn this parable from the fig tree: When its branch has already become tender and **puts forth leaves**, you know that summer is near. 33So you also, when you see all these things, know that it is near—at the doors! Matthew 24:32-33 NKJV*

There have been many commentaries that try to give an explanation for this parable Jesus gives. Most agree that the fig tree represents Israel; however, when it comes to the leaves, they say those must represent the events and signs prior to this passage as a lead-up to Jesus' return. I believe we just received a definitive answer to this parable on August 13th, 2020. Let me explain; the Palestinians implied in their tweet that anyone who acknowledges Israel's existence is a "fig leaf." Ok, as of today, while I'm writing this book, Jordan, Egypt, UAE, Morocco, and Sudan are the only five that have made peace deals with Israel. They represent five fig leaves. It makes sense that if the fig tree represents Israel, the leaves would have to represent those associated with Israel. For example, the "Lion with Eagles Wings" or the "Leopard with Fowl Wings" spoken of in Daniel chapter 7 explained in the first chapter of this book. Furthermore,  Mark's account of the parable of the fig tree found in chapter 13:28-29 is the same as Matthew's account; interestingly, Luke's account is slightly different lets look:

*29Then He spoke to them a parable: "Look at the fig tree, **and all the trees.** 30When they are already budding, you see and know for yourselves that summer is now near. 31So you also, when you see these things happening, know that the kingdom of God is near. Luke 21:29-31 NKJV*

We find from Luke's account that the leaves have been changed to "all the trees." If the fig "tree" represents Israel, which is a "country," then Luke's account suggests that "all the trees" are countries as well. In conclusion, the leaves spoken of by Matthew and Mark are associated with the fig tree as other countries. This is precisely what the Palestinian leadership implied in their tweet as well.

As we continue to see more and more countries making peace deals with Israel, this represents the leaves mentioned here in Matthew 24. Yes, this is a clear sign that Jesus' return is very near, as well as the confirmed covenant that begins Daniel's 70th week! Also, I would like to remind you what God told Daniel in *(Daniel 12:8-9)*, that no one would understand his prophecies until the time of the end. We are now given clues to understanding these Bible prophecies; you just have to pay attention and know your Bible.

More leaves will be springing forth; more countries will have made some kind of peace deal with Israel. This will put tremendous pressure on the Palestinians and the global community that backs them to create a peace deal with Israel; when this happens, the final seven years will have begun, which Daniel 9:27 speaks about. The critical group of people in order for this to come about will be the Palestinians. Why? They have always been the people in a dispute over the land of Israel, specifically Judea and Samaria, the modern-day West Bank, not to mention the city of Jerusalem. Without the Palestinians, you can not have Daniel 9:27.

Israel's persistent endeavor of wanting a peace deal with what appears to be the strongest U.S. backing in recent times as it relates to these peace talks has brought about more discussions by many other nations. Could the Abraham Accords be the one that is ratified or strengthened? It appears to be happening now. A little more time will tell.

I want to point out that Daniel states this covenant will be confirmed with "many" for a week (7 Year Period). I mention this because when a peace deal is signed between Israel and the Palestinians, it will also include many other nations. We know that the Antichrist will be among them, but it doesn't necessarily mean he will be at the forefront. He may be a background figure taking credit along with many other national leaders when this deal is announced and signed; however, without him, it wouldn't have been accomplished. Daniel states we will surely know who he is at the midpoint when the Abomination of Desolation occurs in the newly rebuilt temple. The Abomination of Desolation will be the Antichrist's "big reveal," not at the beginning, as most Bible scholars teach. This will also be when the Antichrist is granted his forty-two months of authority, and the Great Tribulation begins. This answers the question of how the Antichrist is the one who confirms the covenant that Daniel speaks of while also only ruling for 3 1/2 years of it. See the passages below to understand how the dots connect.

15"Therefore when you see the 'abomination of desolation,' spoken of by Daniel the prophet, standing in the holy place" (whoever reads, let him understand).....21 For then there will be great tribulation, such as has not been since the beginning of the world until this time, no, nor ever shall be. Matthew 24:15, 21 NKJV

Jesus clearly states the "abomination of desolation" is the event that will ignite the "great tribulation."

We know from *(Daniel 9:27)* that the abomination of desolation will occur at the midpoint of the final seven-year period, referred to as Daniel's 70th week.

27Then he shall confirm a covenant with many for one week; **But in the middle of the week** *He shall bring an end to sacrifice and offering. And on the wing of* **abominations** **shall be one who makes desolate,** *Even until the consummation, which is determined, Is poured out on the desolate." Daniel 9:27 NKJV*

Jesus says this is the event that ignites the great tribulation spoken of by Daniel the prophet. The first 3 1/2 years of Daniel's 70th week will not be the great tribulation; it doesn't start until the mid-point.

5And he was given a mouth speaking great things and blasphemies, and he was given authority to continue for **forty-two months.** *(3 1/2 years) Revelation 13:5 NKJV*

Also, I would like to point out that Daniel says the confirmed covenant will be seven years. This may or may not be announced as a seven-year deal; the length of the time of this deal may just only last seven years. I can say one thing for sure: if you see a new Jewish Temple being built on the Temple Mount, we are, without a doubt, in the final seven-year period. You shouldn't be left with any confusion at this point, and I suggest you backdate the signing of the Peace Deal and mark it on your calendars. Everything else, as we advance, will be very precise regarding timelines during the final seven-year period. For instance, you can go ahead and mark your calendars 1260 days out (3 1/2 years) from the signing of the deal as when the abomination of desolation will happen and the start of the Great Tribulation. Also, this will mark the arrival of the two witnesses mentioned in Revelation, chapter 11. When announced, this covenant will be followed by a jammed packed seven years full of events (prophecies) culminating at the rapture and 2nd coming of Jesus.

*3For when they say, **"Peace and safety!"** <u>then sudden destruction</u> comes upon them, **as labor pains upon a pregnant woman**. And they shall not escape.*
1st Thessalonians 5:3 NKJV

This passage states that when "they" announce peace and safety, then certain destruction follows. I'm under the conviction that this "destruction" occurs twice. First, during the first 3 1/2 years of the final seven years after the signing of the peace deal, and again after the two witnesses are killed lying in streets mentioned in Revelation chapter 11. They are like book ends or parallels of each other. Let us look at both scenarios beginning with the second one. The  people of the world who take the mark of the beast will be celebrating the two witnesses' deaths proclaiming peace. Three and half days later, the two witnesses resurrect into the clouds, and in that "same hour," the last trumpet sounds, the seventh trumpet. This will be the rapture of the Church, and what follows will be destruction. The whole world will witness what could be almost an hour-long rapture process. Yes, our bodies will be changed in the twinkling of an eye; however, the rapture event itself will be a climatic event unlike any other the entire world will witness with fear and trembling.

*50Now this I say, brethren, that **flesh and blood cannot inherit the kingdom of God**; nor does corruption inherit incorruption. 51Behold, I tell you a mystery: We shall not all sleep, but **we shall all be changed**— 52in a moment, in the <u>twinkling of an eye</u>, **at the last trumpet**. For the trumpet will sound, and the dead **will be raised incorruptible**, and **we shall be changed**. 53<u>For this corruptible must put on incorruption, and this mortal must put on immortality.</u>* 1st Corinthians 15:50-53 NKJV

*For our citizenship is in heaven, from which we also eagerly wait for the Savior, the Lord Jesus Christ, 21**who will transform our lowly body that it may be conformed to His glorious body,** according to the working by which He is able even to subdue all things to Himself. Philippians 3:20-21*

The Bible says in other places that we will ascend into heaven just like Jesus did. Jesus' ascension wasn't in a twinkle of an eye. The "twinkling of an eye" here in 1st Corinthians only references physical transformation. The catching up into the clouds will be seen by everyone, and from what Revelation chapter 11 says, it could be up to an hour-long process that begins with the two witnesses. When Jesus returns to rapture us, it will be much like when he left. People may not see our bodily transformation happen; however, they most certainly will see the rapture event happen! See these passages below.

*9 Now when He had spoken these things, **while they watched**, He was taken up, and a cloud received Him out of their sight. 10 And **while they looked steadfastly toward heaven <u>as He went up</u>**, behold, two men stood by them in white apparel, 11 who also said, "Men of Galilee, why do you stand gazing up into heaven? This same **Jesus**, who was taken up from you into heaven, **will so come in like manner <u>as you saw Him go into heaven</u>**." Acts 1:9-11 NKJV*

ANTICHRIST UNMASKED

*7 Behold, He is coming with clouds, and **every eye will see Him**, even they who pierced Him. And all the tribes of the earth will mourn because of Him. Even so, Amen.*
Revelation 1:7 NKJV

I diverted a bit, talking about the rapture, but I couldn't help it! When they say "peace and safety" the "first time" after the confirmed covenant, we see that the birth pangs mentioned in 1st Thessalonians 5:3 will be intensified with no escape. In other words, events will be much stronger, and nothing will hinder or stop Jesus' arrival, which will be at the conclusion of the final seven years. I can certainly see an upheaval when the Jews can finally worship in their newly rebuilt Temple on the Temple Mount. The Jewish Temple will be included in this covenant as a carrot handed to the Jews to agree on. 1st Thessalonians 5:3 could be referring to the Gog & Magog and the 6th Trumpet war that begins at the Great Euphrates River that will kill one-third of humankind, World War 3. In my book "The EndTime Is Now," I show all the parallels between these two wars spoken of by Ezekiel and Revelation. I've come to believe those two wars are the same. Mankind, after this war, will turn to human answers and his one-world government. League of Nations was established after WW1 and United Nations after WW2, both with the intention of preventing future world wars. After this war, I'm sure it will usher in a full-blown global government led by the Antichrist who stops the sacrifices and commits the Abomination of Desolation. At this point, the Great Tribulation would begin (the midpoint) of the seven-year period. Furthermore (Daniel 8:25) says the Antichrist will use peace to destroy many.

*25And through his policy also he shall cause craft to prosper in his hand; and he shall magnify himself in his heart, **and by peace shall destroy many**: he shall also stand up against the Prince of princes; but he shall be broken without hand. Daniel 8:25 KJV*

Will the Church see the Antichrist before the Rapture?

7For the mystery of lawlessness is already at work; only He who now restrains will do so until He is taken out of the way. 2 Thessalonians 2:7 NKJV

Those that are proponents of the pre-tribulation rapture idea use this verse as their go-to verse. So here they Identify the one who restrains as the Holy Spirit or Church. They interpret this verse as the Antichrist can't be revealed until the Holy Spirit is removed from the earth. Therefore, they are suggesting that because Christians have the Holy Spirit, the Church will also have to be removed (Raptured). They are implying a pre-tribulation Rapture. This all sounds good unless you have identified "He" incorrectly and the meaning of "restrain" incorrectly. Who is "He," and what is meant by restraining? To answer this question, we need to look at this passage in its full context, not just one verse.

*1Now, brethren, **concerning the coming of our Lord Jesus Christ and our gathering together to Him**, we ask you, 2not to be soon shaken in mind or troubled, either by spirit or by word or by letter, as if from us, as though the day of Christ had come. 3Let no one deceive you by any means; **for that Day will not come unless** the falling away comes first, and **the man of sin is revealed**, the son of perdition, 4who opposes and exalts himself above all that is called God or that is worshiped, <u>so that he sits as God in the temple of God, showing himself that he is God.</u> 5Do you not remember that when I was still with you I told you*

*these things? 6And now **you know what is restraining**, that he may be revealed **in his own time.** 7For the mystery of lawlessness is already at work; only He who now restrains will do so until He is taken out of the way. 8**And then the lawless one <u>will be revealed</u>,** whom the Lord will consume with the breath of His mouth and destroy with the brightness of His coming.*
2nd Thessalonians 2:1-8 NKJV

Paul, during his time, was dealing with a lot of distracted Christians who thought during the time that they had missed the rapture. Much like most Christians today believe that Jesus could come back at any moment, they did as well. This is where the doctrine of imminence comes from. Paul rebuked this train of thought right here in this passage. The people were so consumed with whether or not they missed the return of Jesus that they were distracted from doing the work of God. Here Paul basically says, "look, a couple of huge things have to happen before Jesus returns to get us, so get back to work."

We are told from the beginning in verse 1 that this passage is referencing the 2nd coming of Jesus (Rapture). In verse 3, we are told plainly that "this Day will not come unless the falling away comes first, and **that the man of sin is revealed**." Verse 4 here clearly parallels *Daniel 9:27*, the Abomination of Desolation; we already discussed this. When did Daniel say this event was going to happen? In the middle of the seven-year period. The Antichrist can not be revealed globally at any other time, and this passage seems to nail that down. In verse 6, we are given the answer of who "He" is and the meaning of "restraining."

Answer; God and his timing. Many scholars see the phrase "taken out of the way" and automatically want to jump to the conclusion that this means the rapture. God wouldn't tell us one thing a few verses before and then all of a sudden reverse his answer a couple of verses later.

*"God shall judge the righteous and the wicked, For there is a **time** there for every purpose and for every work." Ecclesiastes 3:17 NKJV*

(The entire Ch.3 of Ecclesiastes *is devoted to Timing & God's Timing)*

God controls time. He does everything in His own time; for example, your prayers are answered in His timing. This goes true for the Antichrist and his revealing. **The restrainer is God's timing for the revealing of the Antichrist.** After this event, we know that we have only a short time before Jesus' 2nd coming (Rapture) and the destruction of the Antichrist at the Battle of Armageddon *Vs. 8.*

To conclude, regarding whether the Church will be around to see the Antichrist before the rapture takes place, the answer is a scripturally plainly spoken YES. This passage in 2 Thessalonians answers this question. Clearly, it debunks a pre-tribulation rapture and the doctrine of imminence that Paul was dealing with. First, we know that the rapture can't happen until the Antichrist is revealed globally during the Abomination of Desolation vs. 3-4. Second, that can't happen until the 3 1/2 year point, according to Daniel 9:27. This proof alone puts us already in the middle of the final seven-year period, not at the beginning.

The delusion of a pre-tribulation rapture Satan has managed to convince the Church of may be one of the reasons we see so much evil in our day prevailing. Evil prevails in our day while most Christians sit back and do nothing, waiting

ANTICHRIST UNMASKED

for an "imminent rapture." This was the same thing Paul was dealing with. Pastors and other Bible scholars gloss right over what is plainly spoken and easily understood. What a deception Satan managed to pull off on the Church regarding understanding the Biblical timeline of last-day events. Why fight the escalation of evil when we are about to escape? I don't see the Church restraining anything right now, what I see is evil and the Antichrist system looming larger and more powerful. The sad truth is, for the most part, the modern-day Church is lukewarm. We are not the beautiful bride preparing ourselves for the bridegroom. We soon will be, though. The final seven years, especially the last 3 1/2 years, will put the Church in a place of preparation so that when Jesus comes back, he will receive a spiritually beautiful bride. Pastors are obligated scripturally to warn the Church against evil and possible harm. So that the people of God can prepare themselves accordingly for battle and be the light God intended for us to be during such times.

*And have no fellowship with the unfruitful works of darkness, but rather **expose them**. 12For it is **shameful even to speak of those things which are done by them in secret**. 13But all things that are exposed are made manifest by the light, for whatever makes manifest is light. 14Therefore He says:*

*"**Awake, you who sleep,**
Arise from the dead, And Christ will give you **light**."*
Ephesians 5:11-14 NKJV

The Antichrist will have resistance and opposition.

Of course, it goes without question that Israel will not be a part of the Antichrist system due to the fact the Battle of Armageddon is against Israel led by the Antichrist.

The Church will be an adversary to the Antichrist.

7It was granted to him to make war with the Saints and to overcome them. Revelation 13:7 NKJV

If Antichrist has to war with the Saints, then the Church is posing as a formable adversary. To be clear, there is no such thing as a tribulation Saint and rapture Saint that most pastors and Bible scholars are teaching. This is another unbiblical teaching to defend the pre-tribulation view. The Bible does not say anything anywhere about rapture Saints and then divides the bride into tribulation Saints. There are only Saints. There is only the Church. Some pass before us that are dead in Christ that will rise first, and we who are alive will be caught up in the air. Other than that, there is no such thing as pre-tribulation Saints and then tribulation Saints. There are just only Saints and only the Church. The Church and the Saints are, in fact, synonymous terms.

14And to the woman were given two wings of a great eagle, that she might fly into the wilderness, into her place, where she is nourished for a time, and times, and half a time, from the face of the serpent.
Revelation 12:14 KJV

This passage states that Israel will be given "wings of a great eagle," protecting her for 3 1/2 years from the face of the serpent (Antichrist). We have already spoken in the first chapter about who these wings belong to; it's the United

ANTICHRIST UNMASKED

States. There is a misunderstanding that the eagle's wings here symbolize God's sovereign protection and nothing more. Scholars refer to the symbolic use of eagle wings in *Exodus 19:4* and *Isaiah 40:31* for their rationale. However, as discussed in the first chapter of this book, *Daniel 7:17,23,* Daniel specifically describes to us who these beasts are. Daniel states they are Kings and kingdoms, and we see these beasts mentioned again in Revelation chapter 13 as a cohesive combo beast under the rule of the Antichrist. The Eagles' wings are nowhere to be found because they are here earlier in chapter 12. Therefore to compare *Revelation 12:14* to Exodus or Isaiah is an incorrect analysis based on the detailed information we received from Daniel about these symbols and their meanings during the endtime.

The country of Jordan will not be a part of the Antichrist one-world system either. We know this from *Daniel 11:41.*

41He shall also enter the Glorious Land, and many countries shall be overthrown; but these shall escape from his hand: Edom, Moab, and the prominent people of Ammon. Daniel 11:41 NKJV

All these areas mentioned here are in the country of Jordan. Jordan will never come under the power of the Antichrist.

44But news from the east and the north shall trouble him; therefore he shall go out with great fury to destroy and annihilate many. Daniel 11:44 NKJV

Here, we find that the Antichrist runs into more opposition during the Great Tribulation. He's troubled.

The 2 Witnesses will be adversaries of the Antichrist and cause him problems for the entire 3 1/2 year period.

*3And **I will give power to my two witnesses**, and they will prophesy one thousand two hundred and sixty days, clothed in sackcloth."*
*4These are the two olive trees and the two lampstands standing before the God of the earth. 5And **if anyone wants to harm them, fire proceeds from their mouth and devours their enemies.** And if anyone wants to harm them, he must be killed in this manner. 6These have power to shut heaven, so that no rain falls in the days of their prophecy; and they have power over waters to turn them to blood, and to strike the earth with all plagues, as often as they desire. Revelation 11:3-6 NKJV*

I'm telling you these things because the traditional belief is that the Antichrist will completely control the world without any opposition during the Great Tribulation. Yes, he will be a dominating force worldwide with much power and control; however, he will have to contend with pockets of resistance. The discovery of these pockets of resistance found in the Bible that the Antichrist will have to deal with made me question the meaning of *(Zechariah 14:2)* when it says "all nations" will be coming against Jerusalem at the Battle of Armageddon. This drew me to the conclusion that I explained to you in the first chapter that "all nations" referred to here have to be in reference to a world body that makes the decisions on behalf of all nations, which is now the "United Nations." This will undoubtedly be led by the Antichrist as well. The Good news is that the Antichrist and his partner, the False Prophet, both lose in the end.

*20Then the **beast was captured**, and with him the **false prophet** who worked signs in his presence, by which he deceived those who received the mark of the beast and those who worshiped his image. **These two were cast alive into the lake of fire burning with brimstone.***
Revelation 19:20 NKJV

Below are a vast number of additional characteristics and attributes that are divided into two groups. Some attributes and characteristics only occur during the final seven years, while others can be identified prior.

Antichrist attributes identifiable <u>prior</u> to the final 7 years:

Daniel 7:20 He will look more stout than his fellows
Daniel 8:23 king of fierce countenance
Daniel 8:23 He will be a dark individual, very sinister
Daniel 7:24-25 He will be a man
Daniel 9:26 He will be a Prince
Revelation 17:10-11 He will be preceded by 7 kings he himself will be the 8th.
Isaiah 10:24 He will be of Assyrian descendant or have strong ties with ancient Assyria.
Daniel 7:8 having mouth speaking great things
Daniel 9:27 He will confirm a covenant that last 7 years
Revelation 17:3 He will be a communistic or socialistic government leader (Red spirit)
2 Thessalonians 2;3-4 will claim to be God
2 Thessalonians 2:4 He opposes God
2 Thessalonians 2:4 He claims to be God
Daniel 11:31 Arms shall stand on his part
Daniel 11:38 He will honor the god of fortresses.
Revelation 14:11 Mark of Beast will be a mark of his name
Revelation 15:2 666 will be the number of his name
Revelation 13:18 The number of the beast is 666

2 Thessalonians 2:4 He exalts himself above God
Daniel 11:37 He will not regard the desire of women (No children)
Daniel 11:37 He will not regard the god of his fathers

Antichrist attributes identifiable <u>during</u> final 7 years:

Daniel 7:8 He will arise among 10 kings
Daniel 7:8 He will uproot 3 Kings
Revelation 13:1-2 His 10 nation alliance will converge into a union in which he will rule over.
Daniel 8:25 Will rise on a platform of peace and will destroy many by it
Revelation 13:11-12 He will be elevated by the false prophet
Daniel 8:25 He will cause deceit to prosper
Revelation 13:5 His dominance will last 42 months
Daniel 9:27 Abomination of desolation
Daniel 11:36 He will speak blasphemies against God
2 Thessalonians 2:4 He will set in the Temple of God
Daniel 11:31 He will take away the sacrifices at the time of the Abomination of Desolation
Daniel 11:45 He will plant his tents of his palace between the seas and the glorious holy mountain
Revelation 13:7 He will make war with the Saints
Daniel 7:21, 25 He will make war with Saints for 3 1/2 years
Matthew 24:15, 21 Great tribulation started by the Antichrist
Daniel 7:7 He will rule a terrible strong kingdom
Revelation 13:7 Power was given unto him over all kindreds tongues and nations
Daniel 7:23 shall devour the whole earth.
Daniel 7:25 He will intend to change times and laws
Daniel 8:24 He shall prosper
Daniel 12:7 He will scatter the power of the holy people

Revelation 13:8 all on earth will worship him except those here that are written in the Lambs Book of Life
Revelation 15:2 Antichrist will have an image
2 Thessalonians 2:9 Antichrist comes according to the works of Satan
Revelation 17:14 He will fight against Jesus at the Battle of Armageddon
Daniel 8:25 He will stand against the prince of princes
2 Thessalonians 2:8 The Lord will consume him with the spirit of his mouth
2 Thessalonians 2:8 The Lord will destroy him
Revelation 19:20 Antichrist is cast into lake of fire
Revelation 20:10 Antichrist will be tormented day and night forever and ever

The Antichrist will fulfill everyone one of these attributes listed and all prophecies about him. If he doesn't, he will not be the endtime Antichrist. I've identified at least 51 passages of scripture that provide characteristics. Twenty-one of the 51 passages can be scripturally attributed to the Antichrist right now if he is indeed waiting in the shadows today. That's nearly half of the entire list. Some of these 21 attributes are similar, while others are pretty difficult for someone to meet just one of them. As a matter of fact, there is one characteristic that no one has been able to meet throughout the ages until now.

The spirit of the Antichrist is alive and well today more than ever. I think the person of the Antichrist is here as well on this planet. Things are moving at such a rapid pace. With every crisis, such as the Coronavirus (Undeniable Birth Pang) and this politically motivated green initiative, it appears the global government takes more significant leaps at controlling the masses. They are developing systems that remove more liberties that invade your privacy, all under the guise of the "greater good." The global governance system has been underway for quite some time now, and the Antichrist will soon usurp authority over it to accomplish his will. Based on all the attributes of the Antichrist the Bible list that I have studied more in-depth. I can identify him now and back it up scripturally without contradiction. Yes, several prophecies are yet to be fulfilled concerning the Antichrist that will give us a positive ID as time continues to unfold during the final seven years. It only takes one attribute or prophecy not to align to disqualify a possible candidate. Having said that, what are the odds of a person now who can meet all 21 passages of scripture of the characteristics that could be associated with the Antichrist prior to the final seven-year period? I would say that would be pretty astronomical odds. This is precisely what I intend to show you. Before we get there, we will continue to unmask his plan in the next chapter, Mark Of The Beast. I want you to be thoroughly equipped to know scripturally all about this person and his plans before we attach a name and connect all of these dots.

We have discovered so much scriptural information about the Antichrist and his plans that until now could not be understood entirely. We still have more to uncover. Why would God reveal so much information about this man of sin to us? God wants the last day Saints to recognize our enemy and be spiritually prepared for battle. *"For the lack of knowledge, my people perish"* Hosea 4:6. There have been many great Saints that have passed on to glory before us; however, we are the last generation of Saints that the book of Revelation is speaking towards. Understanding Bible prophecy comes with the blessing of having the foresight to navigate these last days in order to endure till the end. God has given us our game plan and the enemy's playbook through his written word. We have an advantage the wicked will not have during these last days.

Although I heard, I did not understand. Then I said, "My lord, what shall be the end of these things?"
*9And he said, "Go your way, Daniel, for the words are closed up and **sealed till the time of the end**. <u>10Many shall be purified, made white, and refined</u>, but the wicked shall do wickedly; and **none of the wicked shall understand**, but the **wise shall understand**. Daniel 12:8-10 NKJV*

The hard truth is that the final seven years are a time for spiritual purification and refinement for the Church as well as the Jewish people in preparation for the bride to meet her bridegroom in the air. Jesus will not be returning for a spiritually lukewarm Church however a spiritually beautiful Jewish/Gentile bride.

Mark Of The Beast

The Mark of the Beast is described as a multi-facet implementation mechanism that will allow you to function in the economy. We know that it will consist of a "Mark" and pledge system that will require worship to an image of the Antichrist (Revelation 13:15-18).

Many books have been written about the "Great Reset" by some famous people such as Glenn Beck; however, Klaus Schwab, founder of the "World Economic Forum," a globalist tycoon, was the first to write about his plans for the Great Reset. Klaus Schwab is who created that term. He wrote a book titled "Covid 19: The Great Reset." I say all this to say; that if you have read these Great Reset books, then you have read details of a system that has been under development for a while now and is on the fast track presently. The proper name for this system should be called the "Beast System." The only way this system can work is through total compliance.

Revelation shows us a totally compliant economic system utilizing the "mark of the beast."

*16He causes **all**, both small and great, rich and poor, free and slave, to receive a **mark** on their right hand or on their foreheads, 17and that **no one** may buy or sell except one who has the mark or the name of the beast, or the number of his name. 18Here is wisdom. Let him who has understanding calculate the number of the beast, for it is the number of a man: **His number is 666**.*
Revelation 13:16-18 NKJV

For almost the past three years, we have seen for the first time in history global examples or parallels to exactly what Revelation chapter 13:16-18 mention. At first, we were told we had to wear masks everywhere in public and at our workplace. While wearing your mask, you had to be not four, five, seven, or eight feet apart, but coincidently, "6 feet" apart, the Biblical number of man. Without this mask entering into places, you were prohibited from buying and selling. Later this type of conformity escalated. Many nations and even some states and cities throughout the United States prohibited people from buying and selling unless they had a document or digital vaccine passport on their phones. Which coincidentally used trackable QR code technology. For those wondering, the QR codes used in my paperback book are non-trackable and only take you to direct evidential

Video

web-sourced information. QR codes are not the mark of the beast; however, they have been used for nefarious purposes during corona to control behavior. Next, they will want face scans or hand scans before wanting you to be implanted with some sort of tech. Many places in the world still

adhere to these standards and are building from it. You were literally being coerced into putting something into your body that you had little knowledge about. If you did not comply, you became segregated in society, unable to enjoy some freedoms you once held. You just had to trust what the government wanted from you to receive certain freedoms while being told you were contributing to the overall "greater good." The desensitizing and softening campaign by the merchants and governments of the world has been a great success.

One of the last Bible prophecies to occur before Jesus's return that will be implemented worldwide is the "mark of the beast." We are living through the conditioning of such a system right now set forth on a global scale, and the final seven years haven't even begun yet. What really has me rattled is that you don't hear pastors preaching about this. For the most part, they are not warning the Church at all about events the Bible says will be happening during the last days. It just amazes me that in a day where first time last-day prophecies are developing right before our eyes in real-time, the Church is either silent or even promoting these conditioning behaviors.

In this chapter, we will learn more about this beast system and how the Mark of the Beast is now being developed. You will also be surprised to learn that the Bible gives clues as to when the Mark of the Beast will be implemented. The clues have been in the Bible this whole time. Before today, no one could tell you much about the Mark of the Beast, much less the development or what it may even consist of. No one could explain Biblically how such a buying and selling system could be pulled off globally. Sometimes you must live through certain things before you can clearly discern them. I believe this is why God told Daniel in chapter 12 that the prophecies would be sealed till the end and *that the wise would understand.* We are the ones living through the events opening our eyes to a clear understanding of last-day Biblical prophecies. The Bible also states your sons and daughters would be speaking prophecy during the last days, Acts 2:17. This isn't a new prophecy they will be speaking; however, the prophecy that has already been revealed through God's written word.

ANTICHRIST UNMASKED

Simply put, people will come along with a clear understanding of these last-day prophecies that have always been in the Bible. Acts 2:17 seems to indicate that what may have been widely recognized as an understanding of end-time Bible prophecy would need Biblical correction during the last days for clarity and direction due to so much confusion brought about by the various traditional teachings. These Bible prophecies were not meant to be understood entirely and unsealed until the time of the end.

And those of the people who understand shall instruct many... Daniel 11:33 KJV

A message you may have heard concerning the Mark of the Beast 15 years ago would have been a very simplistic sermon with limited information. Information in the Bible from 15 years ago hasn't changed in any way; however, understanding some confusing or complicated passages has now become quite clear and easy to understand. The Bible is alive and breathing today as much as Jesus was the living word 2,000 years ago. We can still get fresh revelation for our times from the Lord through His written word. No other book on the planet is like the Bible. We have the voice of God in our hands, speaking to us during our time! God is omnipotent and omnipresent, and He has given us a book that transcends time. What an awesome God we serve!

16He causes all, both small and great, rich and poor, free and slave, to receive a mark on their right hand or on their foreheads, 17and that no one may buy or sell except one who has the mark or the name of the beast, or the number of his name. Revelation 13:16-17 NKJV

Both the Antichrist and the False Prophet will demand all to follow the one-world government and pledge allegiance to the Antichrist and the one-world religious system; if not, you will face death. The weapon that will be utilized to force all to comply so that they may participate in this economy will be the "mark of the beast." We are closer to this type of system now than anyone may know. The Bible also says that God will forever condemn those that participate in this world economic system utilizing this mark. If everyone is going to be controlled by a mark that includes a number, and you can't buy or sell without it. In that case, we know it will be using technology because it's based on a numbering system. Think about it, right now; all individuals somehow are attached to numbers, for example, Social Security cards, bank accounts, credit cards, driver's licenses, car registration, medical Insurance ID, phone numbers, computer IP addresses, and the list goes on. The difference with the "Mark of the Beast" is that you will be issued a world ID as a mark on/in your person that consolidates all information about you in one place permanently attached to you. I'm going to highlight two main scriptural components of the Mark of the Beast in order for this system to accomplish its goal. While learning about these two main components, you will also learn why God condemns you for taking it. The first component will be a cashless digital component, and the second will be a technological health component.

As of 2017, over 90% of India's population is under an advanced digital system they have created called "Aadhaar ID" and "India Stack." This system uses the biometrics of fingerprints, retina, and face scans connecting everything from welfare benefits to mobile phones. India's

ANTICHRIST UNMASKED

cash was forcibly reduced by 85% and, in turn, forced its people to go into their new digital system. The action of purposely reducing cash forced those into this new digital system. Other countries are also experimenting with chip implants; for instance, Sweden is now chip implanting its citizens in their hands with implants the size of a rice grain to replace cash or credit cards. Over a dozen states in America are getting in front of this and are creating laws to ban chip implantation. This is good for the U.S. and coincides with what we have discussed earlier as the U.S. not being entirely a part of the Antichrist global system and instead supporting Israel.

The examples of India and Sweden look like pilot programs that will be utilized globally in the near future. One component that is still lacking for this to gain traction worldwide is that all countries currently have different types of currency and paper fiat that can't be tracked. Recently the solution being developed to solve this problem is CBDC.

What Is a Central Bank Digital Currency (CBDC)?

Central Bank Digital Currencies are digital tokens comparable to cryptocurrencies issued by a central bank. They depend on the value of that country's currency. Many nations are creating CBDCs, and a few have already implemented them. While many countries are looking for ways to transition to digital currencies, it is essential to understand what they are and what they mean for society.

In the future, "you'll own nothing and be happy." Klaus Schwab, founder and chief executive of the World Economic Forum, says. Schwab's vision is shared by many of the world's richest and most powerful people. They imagine a world where you own nothing. Here's the question. If you own nothing, then who owns everything? The answer is. They own everything.

So how are they going to realize their vision? They will do this through an event called the "Great Reset," which we mentioned in the opening chapter and is underway right now. While this term covers a lot of policy ideas, the focus of the Great Reset is a complete overhaul of the global monetary system. This isn't new. It has occurred before. Since 1900, we have had four global monetary systems – the gold standard, the gold exchange standard, Bretton Woods, and the U.S. fiat dollar standard. On average, each of these systems has had a lifespan of about 40 years. We are now in the 50th year of the U.S. dollar fiat standard, which means we're past due for a new global monetary system. It will likely use a central bank digital currency at its core. If so, governments would gain unprecedented power over individuals. As a matter of fact, at the time of the writing of this book, the Federal Reserve of New York is undergoing a 12-week beta pilot program for CBDC. Participants include some of the largest banks in the United States and world.

In such a system, private bank accounts would disappear. Unlike paper money, which people can privately transact, all transactions will occur in a digital ledger. This means that central bankers will have the ability to view all transactions. Nothing will be private.

The end of paper fiat and its replacement with CBDC will give unlimited power to heads of government. It provides a way to permanently record every financial transaction, and the CBDC

ANTICHRIST UNMASKED

will keep track of where you go and what you do. It will keep track of the websites you visit and the friends you interact with. While most of this information is already available through tracking credit and debit cards, cell phones, and social media profiles. A state-sponsored digital currency would provide uncontrolled access to this information. This would create a closed, government-controlled economic system where everybody depends on the central bank digital currency to participate in society.

This gives the government the ability to control your behavior, down to the most minute details of daily life. If the government decides they don't like you, it can cut off access to your account and kick you out of the economic system. They'll be able to tell you what you can and can't buy. They'll be able to tell you where you can and can't go. They will tell you what vaccines must be administered. They will have total control over your life.

For example, take China's "social credit" system, which establishes a centralized record for individuals and businesses. The system uses a numerical score to punish and reward people and companies based on their economic and personal behavior. Imagine a similar system where you live. The government could punish certain businesses, such as gun shops. Or they could force you to buy celery instead of steak because they "know what's best" for you. The possibilities are infinite. What matters most to central bankers is the ability to manipulate your economic behavior. Today, central banks can print money, but they can't make banks lend money, and they can't make you spend. This means they have no control over currency velocity, an essential part of economic planning. But with CBDCs? They will be able to offer negative interest rates. For example, imagine you have $2,000 worth of CBDCs in your account. Due to slow economic growth and unstable work situation, you choose to save. Central banks want you to spend it and stimulate economic growth. With central bank digital currencies, they can put a negative rate on your account, asking you to spend $2,000 by a specific date or lose 5% to negative interest. For central bankers, it's a tool they've always lacked, giving them direct control over individual behavior. As CBDCs are building their strength, you can be sure they will do whatever it takes to make this happen. We will not be able to avoid them; though the emergence of CBDC is inevitable, we must push back against them vigorously. As long as there are other ways to function in society, we need to use those alternatives.

The Bible says the Antichrist will lead a world government (Revelation 13:17) to control who can buy and who can sell. The Antichrist will need a system that can track every transaction on earth. He will need a way to monopolize all financial transactions and kick people out of the system if they don't do his bidding. The CBDCs create such a system. All that is needed to bring about this "Great Reset" is a global economic crisis like another pandemic or world war. Starving people would gladly adopt such a system if it meant the difference between eating and not eating. We will be assimilated into such a system before cash and credit cards are entirely phased out and before the Mark of the Beast is forced. CBDC's alone are not the mark of the beast. Most people would probably not take a mark on their person right now to function in society; then again, I could be wrong. Anyway, if, for instance, your job were paying you in CBDC instead of fiat currency and you were operating in such a system for a while freely, the government would then have you in a weaker

ANTICHRIST UNMASKED

position of rejecting the mark, which would follow later. In order to keep your job and use your CBDC, you would be forced to get this mark or do without. Sort of like the pilot phase we just went through. Start you off with a mask on your face before we insist you put a substance inside your body. The masks first conditioned you to have something on your person that was very visible. It was not such a significant leap to put something into your body for the same purpose. The mask was meant for; buying and selling, which then carried over to a vaccine being used in the same manner by virtue of "vaccine passports" on phones.

The United Nations also has been promoting the move towards a cashless global society. They have a goal to govern everyone on the planet by 2030. The ID 2020 summit that began in 2020 will be held annually until 2030 with this objective: to number every person on the planet. These efforts are in high gear as we speak.

The Health Component

*11And for this reason God will send them **strong delusion**, that they should believe the **lie**, 12that they all may be **condemned** who did not believe the truth but had pleasure in unrighteousness. 2nd Thessalonians 2:11-12 NKJV*

So from this passage, we see that God will send a "strong delusion" and that anyone who believes "the lie" will be "condemned." It is God that kickstarts the last days because his gracious patience is coming to an end. This delusion is not just any delusion; it's qualified with the word "strong." This delusion will be believable enough for most to fall for and will end in their condemnation or eternal death. This delusion will not be a one-time event or something spoken. The very essence of a delusion is that it will build upon itself to become stronger and more believable over time to deceive many. Having said that, though, the Bible says this delusion will end with a one-time event called "the lie." The delusion that God sends paves the way for those to believe the final lie the Antichrist brings about. In Matthew chapter 24, the Bible speaks of delusions during the last days so strong that even if possible, the very elect could be fooled. The strong delusion is not meant for the Church. This delusion spoken of in 2 Thessalonians and other places will not deceive the elect (Church) because we have been forewarned about it from the Bible. Remember, God told Daniel the wicked would never understand, and it's during these last days whom God's wrath or condemnation will fall upon. Though the Church will be here throughout the final seven years as a witness to the Truth (Jesus Christ), we are shown rejecting this lie that finally comes to fruition. As a result, the Church will not come under the condemnation of God's wrath.

The lie during these last days that will end in condemnation is very easy to discern. It's the Mark of the Beast. The process of getting to this ultimate lie is the "strong delusion." This is a specific lie that is brought about by a specific strong delusion.

Salvation is available to all while we live; however, the Bible says that there will be a time that comes when those who take the "Mark of the Beast" are condemned even while alive.

Then a third angel followed them, saying with a loud voice, "If anyone worships the beast and his image, and **receives his mark on his forehead or on his hand,** *10he himself shall also drink of the wine of the* **wrath of God**, *which is poured out full strength into the cup of His indignation. **He shall be tormented with fire and brimstone** in the presence of the holy angels and in the presence of the Lamb. 11And the smoke of their torment ascends **forever and ever;** and they have no rest day or night, who worship the beast and his image, and **whoever receives the mark of his name.**" Revelation 14:9-11 NKJV*

There have been people who worship Satan and repent and turn their life over to Jesus. Why can't someone turn from Satan and give their life to Jesus after taking the mark? Did you know that the Mark of the Beast is the prophetic sign from the Bible that tells us when God's wrath begins? What year during the final seven years will the Mark of the Beast be doled out? What does this all have to do with the health component of the Mark of the Beast? We will scripturally answer all these tough questions.

The Bible says that the last days will be like the days of Noah. One thing you don't hear many pastors preach about is the Nephilim. They came about through sexual relations between the fallen angels and human women. As a result, the Nephilim were the offspring produced.

*"**The Nephilim** were on the earth both in those days and afterward, when the **sons of God** came to the daughters of mankind, and they bore children to them. Those were the **mighty men of old, men of renown.**" Genesis 6:4 NASB*

The "sons of God" spoken of here in this context refers to the fallen angels. We know this by looking at the book Job.

*6Now there was a day when **the sons of God** came to present themselves before the Lord, **and Satan also came among them**. 7And the Lord said to Satan, "**From where do you come?**" So Satan answered the Lord and said, "From going to and fro on the **earth**, and from walking back and forth on it." Job 1:6-7 NKJV*

In the book of Job, we find that Satan has approached God in heaven along with the "sons of God." Satan was permitted to tempt Job, who was back on earth. What we know here is that Satan wasn't alone. Satan himself is an angel. The "sons of God" were also in heaven, approaching God's throne. These "sons of God" were not earthly. They were with Satan as his angelic followers. This is how we know that Genesis 6:4 refers to fallen angels who caused these women to birth children unlike any other on the planet, Nephilim, the Giants.

We also know that these Nephilim were not human in the sense that God created humankind as. They were part human and part demonic fallen angel. The Nephilim had a tainted DNA. We know that these Nephilim filled the earth and caused all kinds of widespread wickedness to the point God saw it fit to destroy them by the flood.

*And God said to Noah, "The end of all flesh has come before Me, **for the earth is filled with violence through them**; and behold, I will destroy them with the earth. Genesis 6:13 NKJV*

What was Satan trying to do by producing the Nephilim? He was trying to prevent the coming Messiah that would ultimately destroy him. Satan was trying to taint the human bloodline so that Jesus would not be able to be born. God told Satan earlier in Genesis chapter three that there would be one who would come through the seed of the woman that would crush him.

And I will put enmity
Between you and the woman,
And between your seed and her Seed;
He shall bruise your head,
And you shall bruise His heel." Genesis 3:15 NKJV

I believe Satan is up to his old tricks again now, just like in the days of Noah, and that's why the Bible describes the Endtime as such. He is just going about it differently. This time Satan is trying to prevent Jesus' rapture of the Church and his second coming. If there is no one here on the planet to be raptured, then in Satan's mind, he will have foiled God's prophetic plan making God out to be a liar. This is how Satan believes he can win against God and prevent his own demise. This is where the Mark of the Beast comes into play. We know that it will consist of a "Mark" and pledge system that will require worship to an image of the Antichrist (Revelation 13). However, as I mentioned in my previous books, the Mark of the Beast appears to consist of a pharmaceutical composition that could be a future vaccine. We have already lived through how vaccines, for the first time on a global scale, are being used to make people conform to a new way of living.

Like in the Days of Noah, Satan plans to attack humanity once again at the genetic DNA fingerprint level of God's crown jewel of creation. It's going to be through a series of synthetic vaccines that will end with the final vaccine, the end-all of vaccines, the last one you will ever need. I'm sure this is how it will be pitched anyway. I've discovered some additional scriptural information that re-enforces this thought and pinpoints the primary tool of deception used to drive humanity to the Mark of the Beast.

*".....For your **merchants** were the great men of the earth, for by your **sorcery** all the nations were **deceived**. Revelation 18:23 NKJV*

The word "Sorcery" used here, the original language of the Greek New Testament, is the Greek word "Pharmakeia." Pharmakeia means "drugs." This appears five times in the New

Testament. We also get our English word pharmacy from the Greek word Pharmakeia. The context here is about the headquarters of the False Prophet, "Mystery Babylon," being destroyed at the end of the tribulation period; however, there is a reflection moment made here. Notice that "all" nations were "deceived" by sorcery "Pharmakeia." Interestingly, according to the strong's concordance, the context in which "sorcery" is used in the original Greek is *"the use or administering of drugs."* By replacing the word sorcery with its actual Greek usage in Revelation 18:23, it would read like this:

*".....For your **merchants** were the great men of the earth, for by your **administering of drugs** all the nations were **deceived**." Revelation 18:23*

The "strong delusion" and "lie" of
2nd Thessalonians 2:11-12 would not contradict this. I believe the strong delusion started in 2020 and will be restated and repeated constantly until the fulfillment of this grand lie from the father of lies that culminates with the "Mark of the beast." As of the writing of this book, people are already on their 4th or 5th corona mRNA booster shot which indicates the vaccine is not a vaccine. The merchants (businesses) are being used today to perpetrate this lie along with their government leaders of the world. This couldn't have been pulled off 2,000 years ago when this was written; however, for the first time in history, we see all nations in lockstep today with Pharmakeia (false vaccine) for the purpose of deceiving, not healing. Watch and listen to Yuval Noah Harari, the number one advisor to Klaus Schwab, founder of the World Economic Forum.

Video

After being administered with the complexity of what this "Mark" intel's, I believe that just like in the Days of Noah, Satan tampers with God's fingerprints of human DNA. In turn, after administering this final piece of the puzzle (false vaccine), it converts you into something other than what God had initially created humankind as on the molecular DNA level. Therefore becoming forever condemned and unable to undo.

Am I saying that anyone that takes the Mark of the Beast their whole DNA structure will be changed? NO. You would only need 1% of your DNA changed to no longer be considered human. Take, for instance, a chimpanzee's DNA and humans. There is less than a 15% difference between both, yet look at what change it produces. It's not the similarity between different species' DNA that's important because we have all been created by one artist whose signature is on all creation. It's the minor differences in our DNA that makes each living creature so unique between each other. 1% is all Satan needs to accomplish to ruin humankind's DNA, making us no longer human in the sense that God created humanity as.

You may not think a simple shot or series of shots could do something like changing your DNA; however, this first synthetic vaccine being administered today does add messenger "m" to your RNA (mRNA), which works closely with your DNA. For example, if you cut yourself, your DNA tells your RNA that a problem must be fixed. Furthermore, Transgender people take a series of shots that work to reconstruct their hormones and balances, etc. This type of mRNA medical technology is being used today on humans on a global scale. It will continue to be perfected to the point that it will alter your DNA

ANTICHRIST UNMASKED

with no mitigating alternatives. You will not be able to reverse the outcome. We are living through the development of the lie now being perpetrated on humanity through a series of lies that will end at the ultimate lie, the "mark." Terms like "Trans-humanism, Human 2.0, godlike, and Superhuman" will be heard more frequently as these globalists continue to sell the idea of merging technology with humans for the 'greater good.' Pharmakeia will be the number one component of this technology.

*You are of your father the devil, and the desires of your father you want to do. He was a **murderer** from the beginning, and does not stand in the truth, because **there is no truth in him**. When he speaks a lie, he speaks from his own resources, **for he is a liar and the father of it.** John 8:44 NKJV*

As of the writing of this book, no one has taken the Mark of the Beast. You will not accidentally take the Mark of the Beast. The Antichrist has yet to be revealed, and he has no authority at the moment. The Mark of the Beast can only be implemented once the Antichrist is ruling. We know this because it will consist of the number of his name mentioned in Revelation chapter 13. Whoever is marked will be like a slave with ownership belonging to Satan.

The three main components that make the Mark of the Beast so recognizable are the economic component of buying & selling through a cashless trackable token, the health component, and a pledge of worship to this global leader the Bible calls the Antichrist 666. All three of these will be wrapped up in one package in order for anyone to be able to function in society. To anyone who takes this mark, your free will is eliminated. God gave humankind free will, and Satan will be taking it away. The instant free will is eliminated globally by using this mark; God

ANTICHRIST UNMASKED

will intervene. The timing of God's wrath begins immediately after the administration of the Mark of the Beast.

*"1Then I heard a loud voice from the temple saying to the seven angels, "Go and pour out the **bowls of the wrath of God** onto the earth." 2So the **first** went and poured out his bowl upon the earth, and a **foul and loathsome sore** came upon the **men who had the mark of the beast and those who worshiped his image."** Revelation 16:2 NKJV*

This gives us a timeline of when God's wrath will be poured out on humanity. God's wrath doesn't begin until after the administering of the Mark of the Beast. The fact that foul-smelling sores come upon people who take the "Mark of the Beast" appears to be a pharmaceutical or medical reaction that causes these effects. This is why we can connect the dots between Revelation 18:23, "Mark of the Beast," and a pharmaceutical vaccine. There will be a smelly, visibly contrasting difference between those who have taken the mark and those who have not. This will indeed be the zombie apocalypse.

It's only during the endtime when people take the "Mark" that they become forever condemned. For example, during the tribulation period prior to the Mark of the Beast being administered, people will worship the Antichrist in this one-world religion led by the false prophet. But God saves many out of this false religion right before the Mark of the Beast is administered and his wrath is poured out.

*And I heard another voice from heaven saying, **"Come out of her my people"**, lest you share in her sins, and **lest you receive of her plaques.** Revelation 18:4 NKJV*

We know the timing of God's wrath when we see the Mark of the Beast administered; however, when will the Mark of the Beast be administered? Does the Bible tell us? Actually, it does. We get the answer going back to the book of Genesis. Jesus says in Mathew that his coming will be a time like the days of Noah.

"37But as the days of Noah were, so also will the coming of the Son of Man be. Mathew 24:37 NKJV

4For after seven more days I will cause it to rain on the earth forty days and forty nights, and I will destroy from the face of the earth all living things that I have made." Genesis 6:4 NKJV

We know that Noah was given a seven-day notice ahead of time of the day of his departure and the wrath of God. God's wrath during the Days of Noah didn't occur until the 7th day. God's wrath during the final seven years will not happen until the 7th year. Traditional teaching is that the entire final seven-year period is God's wrath being poured out on humanity, and because Christians are not appointed unto God's wrath, we will be raptured before it begins. Though we as Christians aren't appointed unto God's wrath, the mistake made by scholars and pastors is in the details and understanding of God's word concerning this topic matter. Some coin the phrase, why would God beat his bride before the wedding? God will not beat his bride but instead will receive a spiritually beautiful bride that will endure till the end like Noah. The absolute truth here is that the "Great Tribulation" is not God's wrath; it's Satan's wrath. There are several passages to show this; here is one example.

25He shall speak pompous words against the Most High,
Shall persecute the Saints of the Most High,
And shall intend to change times and law.
Then the Saints shall be given into his hand
For a time and times and half a time
(3 1/2 years).... Daniel 7:25 NKJV

Let me be abundantly clear that the "Great Tribulation" is not God's wrath; it's Satan's wrath. God's wrath does not begin until the very end of the seven-year period. The seven bowls are filled up with the "wrath of God." Most of the wrath of God is poured out at the "Battle of Armageddon." We, as the Gentile Christians, along with the 144,000, are sealed for protection during the time of God's wrath, much like the Jews were protected before being exiled from Egypt. They placed blood on their doorpost, and the death angel passed over them. They did not suffer from the plagues God sent upon Pharaoh and Egypt. The Jews were exiled after the ten plagues, and we will be redeemed at the final seventh bowl. Those of us who are Christians are sealed by the blood of Christ until the day of redemption. We will know our redemption is extremely close when God's wrath begins.

*13In Him you also trusted, after you heard the word of truth, the gospel of your salvation; in whom also, having believed, **you were sealed with the Holy Spirit** of promise, 14who is the guarantee of our inheritance **until the redemption of the purchased possession**, to the praise of His glory. Ephesians 1:13-14 NKJV*

It has been speculated through calculation of the time frame of each plague brought onto Egypt that it only took approximately thirty days for all ten plagues to transpire. When this Mark of the Beast is administered, and Satan believes he has his system in place. God will dismantle it quickly through these seven bowls that will parallel many of the plagues brought upon Egypt. Those who will have taken this mark to function in this new society will have been deceived and receive no benefit of being a part of it. They will instead inherit an eternal death in the lake of fire. Satan's game plan has always been deception.

Jesus's first warning to those living during the last days is, *"Take heed that no one deceives you"* Mathew 24:4. Eve's response to God in the garden was, *"The serpent deceived me, and I ate."* Genesis 3:13.

What we went through with Covid was a test trial of a new system. Later down the road, they will come harder and stronger using something else, such as another pandemic, Climate Change initiatives, or World War. Maybe a combination of all of the above. This will eventually lead to the ultimate control in eliminating free will by implementing the Mark of the Beast. "Power corrupts, and absolute power corrupts absolutely." This statement couldn't be more true today.

The platform of the Antichrist is in high gear now and moving closer to completion every day. Many antichrist figures such as Yuval Noah Harari, Klaus Schwab, Bill Gates, Elon Musk, King Charles III, and many others are preparing the way for the ultimate Antichrist to take the reign. The system in place at the time will be what the Antichrist and False Prophet usurp authority over. The Antichrist and False Prophet will be "holding hands," so to speak, to force conformity into this socialistic system.

My rule of thumb is that I will never allow anything on or in my person to function in society, no tattoo, invisible tattoo, chip, micro nanotechnology, etc. This is evil and an evil that needs to be rejected!

ANTICHRIST UNMASKED

Hebrew Biblical Calendar

L et's talk about the Hebrew Biblical calendar. This calendar is considered the Biblical calendar. The calendar begins on Rosh Hashanah, which happens in September, and ends the following September of the next year. This calendar keeps in sync with the natural cycles of the sun and the moon. Rosh Hashanah is each Biblical calendar year's first day or new year. Because they start their calendar on year 1 of Biblical creation, according to Jewish calculations, at the time of the writing of this book, we are currently in the year 5783. The calendar we use is called the Gregorian calendar, which is only based on the cycles of the sun.

So you may ask, what's so important about this Jewish Hebrew calendar, considered the Biblical calendar? Christians need to get on the Biblical calendar to understand God's calendar. He set this up from the beginning. God doesn't operate off our calendar. All the Biblical feasts and holidays are based on the Hebrew calendar.

*"To everything there is **a season, A time** for **every purpose under heaven:**" Ecclesiastes 3:1 NKJV*

*"But **concerning the times and the seasons**, brethren, you have no need that I should write to you. For you yourselves know perfectly that the **day of the Lord so comes as a thief in the night.** For when they say, "Peace and safety!" then sudden destruction comes upon them, as*

*labor pains upon a pregnant woman. And they shall not escape. **But you, brethren, are not in darkness, so that this Day should overtake you as a thief.** You are all sons of light and sons of the day. **We are not of the night nor of darkness.***"
I Thessalonians 5:1-5 NKJV

Another unique observation about this calendar is that it's based on a seven-year cycle. The seventh year of every cycle is considered a Shmita year, known as the year of release. We just finished a Shmita year. This year began in September 2021 and ended on September 25th, 2022. September 26th of, 2022 was Rosh Hashanah, the first day of the new year. This means that beginning September 26th, we began the first day of the year of a new Biblical seven-year cycle.

Another exciting thing about this year is that it is also a jubilee year. A jubilee year occurs after seven cycles of seven years (49 years); the following year is considered a jubilee year, the 50th year. The jubilee year begins on the 10th day of the new year, which this year was on October 5th 2022. The holiday that falls on this day is Yom Kipper. Another interesting thing to note is that according to many Jewish theologians, the 1st Temple was destroyed in the year 3382, which was a Jubilee year. If you divide by 49, this is how you know if the first year of the next seven-year cycle is a jubilee year. So using this, we know that the 1st Temple was destroyed on the 69th Jubilee. October 5th of this year would be 5782 / 49 = 118th Jubilee. This will be the 49th Jubilee since the 1st Temple was destroyed.

OK, I'm going to try to wrap this up. This September 26th, we began a new seven-year cycle. This first Biblical calendar year is also a jubilee that only occurs once every 50 years. We have started a seven-year cycle that includes a jubilee year that has also began the next jubilee cycle towards the 50th jubilee after the first temple was destroyed. This is huge!

I consider right now, through the end of 2023, a high watch year for not the Church's rapture but instead the beginning of Daniel's 70th week found in Daniel 9:27. One caveat to consider, though, is that Rosh Hashanah is celebrated not at the beginning of the actual Hebrew calendar. It's actually celebrated on the 6th month of the Hebrew calendar. I know this sounds confusing. The reason the Jews celebrate their New Year on the 6th month is that it is supposed to symbolize and correlate to the 6th day of creation when man (Adam) was created, and authority was given from God to man on that day. The actual end of this first year based on the Hebrew calendar "months" wouldn't end until April 7th, 2024, on the Gregorian calendar. This month is "Adar II," in which a 13 month are added because of leap years. Nissan is the first month on the Hebrew calendar, which began on March 22nd, 2023, on the Gregorian calendar. Though I'm in no way dogmatic, this is just speculation on my part; if Rosh Hashanah comes and goes, just keep in mind that this first year based on Hebrew months doesn't end until April 7th, 2024, on the Gregorian calendar.

*"Then **he shall confirm a covenant with many** for **one week**; But in the middle of the week He shall bring an end to sacrifice and offering. And on the wing of abominations shall be one who makes desolate, Even until the consummation, which is determined, Is poured out on the desolate." Daniel 9:27 NKJV*

Daniel was a Jew, and the end time confirmed covenant by the Antichrist that Daniel is speaking about is a week of years, a seven-year period. Are you seeing where I'm headed with this? Daniel's 70th week or final seven years of the end of this age would have to fall into one of these 7-year cycles. So if we don't see the confirmation of the covenant between Israel/Palestinians that will also include many other nations this upcoming year between now and 2023 or early 2024, then that means the final seven years will not have another opportunity to occur until 2030 in order for Daniel's 70th week or final seven years to fit perfectly into a Biblical seven-year cycle. I will say again I'm not entirely dogmatic on this. Interestingly, the globalist leaders of the United Nations and World Economic Forum, etc., have a date set forth to accomplish their goals by 2030. It's called the 2030 agenda. What a coincidence.

Daniel's 70th week, when it commences, will begin our journey to the Church's rapture that will occur on the 7th year, a Shmita year, the year of release!

One last thing that's pretty mind-blowing! One component left out when the Jewish theologians calculated and created the calendar based on Biblical years is that they left out the time they believe the Israelites were actually in Egypt. Rashi, who was a rabbi, is one of the most influential Jewish commentators in history. According to "Rashi's commentary," the Israelites were in Egypt for only 210 years. This is the sum one comes to when counting the lifespans of Jacob, Levi, Kohath, Amram, and Moses" of who begat who.

If the Jewish calculations are correct, September 26th, 2022, began the year 5783 according to the Jewish Hebrew Biblical calendar; however, if you put back the 210 years lost into this calendar, that puts us at year 5993 with only seven years left to conclude the 6,000th year!!

5783 + 210 = year 5993

"But, beloved, do not forget this one thing, that with the Lord one day is as a thousand years, and a thousand years as one day." II Peter 3:8 NKJV

God has a 7 thousand year plan that parallels the seven days of creation. We are quickly coming to the end of the sixth thousandth year now. The 7th day of rest will be Jesus' millennium reign in the following one thousand years.

This past Shmita year was full of surprises: The Russian Bear has risen in war, Rowe vs. Wade after 50 years has been overturned here in the United States, wars and rumors of wars are at levels not seen since world war 2. Keep a watchful eye because this current jubilee year, we may be in store for some events on a Biblical scale not experienced since Jesus was here 2,000 years ago!

For those familiar with replacement theology, I don't adhere to that sort of false doctrine. I believe God will deal with the Jews during the final 3.5 years of Jacob's trouble. Let me remind you that we serve a big God who can do more than one thing at a time. In the early Church, there was a Jewish/Gentile mixed Church. When Jesus comes to receive his bride in the clouds, known as the 1st resurrection, Jesus will again return for a Jewish/Gentile mixed Church. This is what the Bible clearly teaches.

*4And I saw thrones, and they sat on them, and judgment was committed to them. Then I saw the **souls** of those who had been **beheaded for their witness to Jesus and for the word of God**, who had not worshiped the beast or his image, and had not received his mark on their foreheads or on their hands. **And they lived and reigned with Christ for a thousand years**. 5But the rest of the dead did not live again until the thousand years were finished. **This is the <u>first resurrection</u>. 6Blessed and holy is he who has part in the <u>first resurrection.</u>** Over such the second death has no power, but **they shall be priests of God and of Christ, and shall reign with Him a thousand years.***
Revelation 20:4-6 NKJV

There is no debate among most scholars and pastors that the 1st resurrection is the rapture of the Church. The problem is that pre-trib proponents skip over passages that contradict the traditional teachings they have been taught in seminary. This passage plainly shows us that those that are beheaded for their witness to Jesus and who did not receive the mark of the beast are a part of the first resurrection. These people that are beheaded are also mentioned as reigning with Christ during the 1,000-year millennium that follows. How could those who did not receive the mark of the beast and were beheaded be a part of the rapture (1st resurrection) if it happened seven years prior?

During the tribulation, it describes those who died for the faith and those who came through the tribulation as part of the 1st resurrection. There is only one 1st resurrection, and it's the rapture. This didn't happen seven years prior.

I know I've digressed a little here; however, this topic has to be cleared up, and this is good of a place as any. Most that hold a post-trib rapture view are often accused of being "replacement

ANTICHRIST UNMASKED

theology" teachers or false teachers that eliminate the Jews and God's plan for them during the last days. Maybe this holds true for some. I really have a problem with labels being placed on whole groups of people that aren't true to close debates on topics concerning eschatology. I'm a layman, and I read and study God's word for myself and use the gift of discernment that God gives me to find the truth. The truth is God does have a plan for the Church and the Jews have always been a part of it. There is no separation between the Jew and the Church. I submit that the Jews were, in fact, the first members of God's Church, before even the Gentiles. Because the Jews later rejected Jesus, God still has to deal with his chosen people before the millennium kingdom being set up. God will simultaneously deal with the Jewish people and the lukewarm Gentile Church during the final seven years. Daniel 12:9-10 says the Church will be purified, made white, and refined.

*16For I am not ashamed of the **gospel of Christ**, for it is the power of God to salvation for **everyone** who believes, for the **Jew first** and also for the Greek.*
Romans 1:16 NKJV

I'm going to close this topic out here with two more passages.

*9After these things I looked, and behold, **a great multitude which no one could number**, of **all nations**, <u>tribes, peoples, and tongues</u>, standing before the throne and before the Lamb, clothed with white robes, with palm branches in their hands Revelation 7:9 NKJV*

*13Then one of the elders answered, saying to me, "**Who are these** arrayed in white robes, and **where did they come from?**"*

14And I said to him, "Sir, you know."
*So he said to me, **"These are the ones who <u>come out</u> of the great tribulation**, and washed their robes and made them white in the blood of the Lamb.*
Revelation 7:13-14 NKJV

Revelation chapter 7, at the end of the tribulation, shows us both the Jewish Church and the Gentile Church out of every nation, tribe, peoples, and tongue seen suddenly together in heaven. Just like the Jews and the Gentiles were together in the early Church Age. All seen here have been sealed for the one and only day of redemption, the Rapture. When Jesus comes to receive his Church which includes the Jews, Jesus will return for a fully "spiritually" beautiful bride, not bride's plural.

*25For I do not desire, brethren, that you should be ignorant of this mystery, lest you should be wise in your own opinion, that **blindness in part** <u>has happened to Israel until the fullness of the Gentiles has come in</u>. 26And so **all Israel will be saved**, as it is written:"The Deliverer will come out of Zion, And **He will turn away ungodliness from <u>Jacob</u>**; Romans 11:25-26 NKJV*

This verse perfectly describes God simultaneously dealing with the Jews and the Gentiles (*you and me*) during the tribulation. Some Jews will continue to reject Jesus until what the Bible says, *"until the fullness of the Gentiles has come in."* When this happens, those Jews still alive during the tribulation (*the time of Jacob's trouble, finale 3 1/2 years*) will be saved. What does it mean by "until the fullness of the Gentiles come in?" **Answer:** It's when the last Gentile accepts Christ, who is a part of the rapture. The next question would be when will this happen? People are constantly being born as the next Gentile to be reached. **Answer:** It's when the Great Commission ceases. It's when the ministry of the Gospel of Christ is over. When will this happen? **Answer:** At the time of the administering "Mark of the Beast," we learned that this is when God's wrath begins with the 7 bowls. In conclusion, God will deal with the Jews and the Gentiles throughout the entire tribulation period. It will be the most remarkable revival this world has ever had.

I get so excited about the rapture. I know some look at Daniel 9:27 as a marker for the most terrible time in human history; however, the reality is we will only be seven years from the rapture when this event happens. That's something as believers to get excited about. God didn't give us a heart of fear (2 Timothy 1:7). The  Church has been waiting for 2,000 years for Jesus's return. When I see this event finally happen, I will know that my redemption is drawing nearer than ever before. 1st Thessalonians 4:13-18 will become so real during this time. It will be what I believe will  spawn a revival among the Church to the likings that this world has not ever seen. During the final seven years, this world will witness the most remarkable revival of the Church ever, causing Antichrist to have to war against the Saints. We will be a formable resistance against Satan as the Church continues on a high level full of the Holy Spirit to fulfill the Great Commission during the Great Tribulation. This will be the best of times and worst of times all at the same time.

Personally, I can't wait to see all Christians on the same page concerning eschatology. As events continue to transpire, God will drive all Christians to the undeniable truth concerning this topic. When this happens, we will be a force to reckon with. The sooner, the better. I'm looking forward to my brothers and sisters to start connecting the eschatological dots. This is

ANTICHRIST UNMASKED

the primary reason I've written the books I have written. It seems that the beast system is being established now unabated without any "restraining" because pastors aren't warning and advising the flock Biblically in addressing all the evil transpiring in our world today. Instead, it seems the Church is just an onlooker of what Satan is accomplishing at unprecedented prophetic speed. For the most part, the Church is being told that things happening now are shadows of the coming tribulation, so therefore the rapture is about to occur anytime without any further events that need to happen. This "opinion" is unbiblical. Do you think this kind of message inspires the Church to fight evil as the Bible commands? Maybe a Christian rather allow evil to continue to take over the world while falsely believing that doing so will usher in the rapture sooner. In a later chapter, we will discuss our Biblical mandate and how to be prepared during these last days.

I hope this brief study of the Hebrew Biblical calendar gives you something to ponder. I am not an expert on this topic, and I find it very intriguing and interesting.

Unmasked

This is the chapter that we have been building up to. I hope you have not skipped to this chapter without reading and understanding what was learned in the previous chapters. This is where many dots start connecting. We have already learned when the "man of sin" will be revealed globally. This will be at the 3 1/2 year mark of the final seven years of Daniel's 70th week, not at the beginning as most scholars and pastors teach. Though you will be learning in this chapter the name of the person of the Antichrist, this is in no way the revealing mentioned in 2nd Thessalonians chapter two, which indicates that the Antichrist's revealing "globally" will be at the abomination of desolation. For those "watching," we can still identify him during the last days prior to the abomination of desolation due to all the information and clues the Bible tells us to look for. Though the Antichrist has the primary hand in confirming the false covenant that begins the final seven years, he will not be revealed or given authority until the 3.5-year mark. At the beginning of the final seven years, as we discussed earlier, Antichrist will be a leader among many taking credit for this false covenant. After the destruction that follows (War), Antichrist will begin to rise to global power with the help of the False Prophet (Pope) during the first 3.5 years, which will result in him being granted authority to rule the remaining 3.5 years. This will begin the Great Tribulation.

In the "Antichrist chapter," I showed you two lists of characteristics and attributes of the final Antichrist. One list shows us characteristics that could be applied to this person if he is currently waiting in the shadows of the final seven years that are on the brink of beginning now. The second list shows us attributes that only can be applied to him after the final seven years commences. I'm going to show you how all of the characteristics from the Bible that list Antichrist attributes applied to him prior to the seven years point to only one person on the planet right now. There are even a couple of attributes we can borrow from the second list that this person is already mentioning verbatim with his mouth that brings prophetic scripture to life.

The odds that one individual right now matches all 21 passages referenced about his characteristics are astronomical; keep in mind some of these attributes have many moving parts, which makes the probabilities even more off the charts. As I stated earlier, he is already speaking life into some of the events that will take place on the 2nd list of attributes that will be fulfilled during the final seven-year period. In 16 bullet points, we will be correlating 25 passages of scripture that point to only one person today. This is why I'm so confident writing this book unmasking this person. Whether now or later, I hope it will be helpful to the Saints (the Church) in opposing and navigating the times in which we live. When you know certain events are coming and you have the playbook of your enemy, you can prepare accordingly to endure the battle until the end. Bible prophecy gives the Church the ability to continue to get the gospel out to as many people as possible during the Great Tribulation that we will have to endure. The Antichrist is not mentioned in the Bible making war with the Saints for nothing. We will be strong adversaries against him being led by the Holy Spirit, Bible, and the two witnesses God sends.

My intention is not to give you an exhaustive list of current global leaders and start drawing comparisons to eliminate them one by one. It is much easier to disqualify a person as Antichrist than to prove otherwise. It only takes one Biblical characteristic not to match to eliminate a person. My original plan in writing this book was to focus on the one and only person it can be and connect all the dots scripturally to unmask him. I had no intention of talking about any other possible candidates. I say all of this to say that while I was writing this book, the rumor mills started flying about Prince Charles III. He became King Charles III once Queen Elizabeth passed away and became the number one contender for the title of Antichrist. So to dispel any doubts about who I'm Biblically going to prove to you who Antichrist is, I'm first going to show you how easy it is to disqualify someone by using King Charles III as an example. Let's begin.

With the passing of Queen Elizabeth, the world continues to change. Pawns are being placed strategically. Leadership shifts in the world are happening unexpectedly, especially in Europe.

England now has a King. Prince Charles III instantly became King after the passing of Queen Elizabeth. On the heels, Great Britain, a few days prior, getting a new Prime Minister, Liz Truss, due to the sudden stepping down of Boris Johnson. Liz Truss's reign was the shortest in UK history.

A few folks have asked me whether or not the now King Charles III could possibly be Antichrist. Apparently, a lot is going around on the internet concerning a Biblical characteristic here and there, and even some sensational things added like a "pure bloodline," etc. I can tell you with Biblical clarity that King Charles III is not the Antichrist. This doesn't mean his new role as King will not play a significant role in the last days. I believe what's transpiring is very substantial, and the time clock is quickly ticking away ever so closer to the approach of the final seven-year period.

We are not waiting for the book of Revelation to begin to unfold; we have been for a while living through the book of Revelation as it ever so closely draws us nearer to the Beast system led by the Antichrist himself at the 3 1/2 year point of Daniel's 70th week.

You need to understand that Antichrist has to fulfill every Biblical qualification about him, or he can't be the last days' Antichrist. There are over 50 Biblical characteristics mentioned about the Antichrist in the Bible. Though someone can always attribute one or two characteristics to someone doesn't mean that person is Antichrist. Allow me to show you Biblically how Prince Charles III is quickly disqualified with just one attribute.

The Antichrist will not regard the desire of women.

*"Neither shall he regard the God of his fathers, **nor the desire of women**, nor regard any god: for he shall magnify himself above all." Daniel 11:37 KJV*

Some interpretations are that this must mean Antichrist has to be gay. If this is true, King Charles has never demonstrated any such behavior that we know of. Also, another interpretation that I lean more towards is that this would mean the Antichrist would not have any children of his own. After all, what do most women desire? Children. So the Antichrist, not

ANTICHRIST UNMASKED

regarding the desire of women, would mean no children of his own. I wouldn't expect Antichrist to share his glory with offspring, so this seems to make more sense. King Charles III has two children, Prince William and Prince Harry. Either way, you want to interpret this particular Antichrist characteristic, King Charles III doesn't fit; therefore, he is disqualified as a potential Antichrist candidate.

Prince Charles III, now assuming the role of King, carries significant Biblically prophetic implications. Here's why, in the chapter about the Four Beast, each beast represents a last day's kingdom, as Daniel describes. These kingdoms' symbols would have to relate to nations on the planet during the last days. One of these kingdoms is the Lion (Great Britain). Later in John's Revelation, we see these four Beast kingdoms again as one cohesive combo beast representing the Antichrist's final United Kingdom. The Lion is mentioned with an emphasized attribute. It states he has a "mouth of a lion."

*"And the beast which I saw was like unto a leopard, and his feet were as the feet of a bear, **and his mouth as the mouth of a lion:** and the dragon gave him his power, and his seat, and great authority." Revelation 13:2 KJV*

King Charles III may be one of the future's primary mouthpieces, bidding for the continuation of the development of this new global beast system and carrying on later as a megaphone for the Antichrist.

King Charles is a massive proponent of world government and has made some bold eyebrow-raising statements recently. At the "UN Climate Change Conference UK 2021," he made this statement below.

Video

*"We need a vast military-style campaign to marshal the strength of the global private sector with trillions at **his** disposal,"* You can also find his comments on video from the internet.
See video

This entire comment is disturbing, and he attributed this to some lone male figure's disposal. Was this a slip of the tongue or the truth? This was a completed thought, not a misstated word. He was reading from a script.

King Charles III states he wants to gather all the assets in the world (trillions) for "his" disposal. In the name of climate change, he is advocating for a military-style campaign to take over the private sector. He wants to garner all power consolidated into one individual. King Charles wasn't referring to himself when he made this comment; it was someone else.

Climate change, Covid, Monkey Pox, War, etc., are all distractions for this "one" individual to eventually garner absolute power. King Charles may very well know who that one may be. So to close, I say all this to say let's see what the mouth of the lion says going forward. King Charles doesn't appear to be quiet and to himself like Queen Elizabeth.

Something else I find interesting about King Charles III is that his very first diplomatic visit as King is to a nation and its leader, who is the Antichrist candidate I'm unmasking in this book. Who will King Charles III be visiting first as King? None other than Emmanuel Macron, President of France. As a matter of fact, a lot of new leaders have been making visits to see Emmanuel Macron lately. The new United Arab of Emirates President, Sheikh Mohamed bin Zayed first official state visit after assuming office was with

Emmanuel Macron. Saudi Crown Prince Mohammed bin Salman has met with Emmanuel Macron several times and visited again with Emmanuel Macron in July of 2022. Interim Prime Minister Yair Lapid's first diplomatic visit days after taking office was in France with Emmanuel Macron. They held talks toward establishing peace with the Palestinians. Mahmoud Abbas, the Palestinian leader, met with Emmanuel Macron following Prime Minister Yair Lapid's visit. What was interesting is that all of these middle eastern leaders met with Emmanuel Macron just days apart from each's visit in July of 2022. Macron wasted no time inviting the newly re-elected Prime Minister Benjamin Netanyahu of Israel to France following the November 2022 elections.

The unusual activity in July of primarily new leaders all making their first diplomatic visits within close proximity of each other with Emmanuel Macron went nearly unnoticed. It's like they know he is the point man for advisory council. Now we have the newly assumed role of King Charles III doing the same thing. The first diplomatic visit he is making is with non-other than Emmanuel Macron. Is Emmanuel Macron the person King Charles III was referencing in his speech at the "UN Climate Change Conference UK 2021" when he mentioned that "trillions would be at his disposal?" Also, two months after those July visits with all of those middle eastern leaders, we have former Prime Minister Yair Lapid announcing at the United Nation's general assembly on September 22, 2022, that a two-state solution with the Palestinians would be good for Israel's "security" and that every Muslim nation should "recognize" their existence.

MBS

Yair Lapid

Abbas

Netanyahu

Video

ANTICHRIST UNMASKED

Now that Benjamin Netanyahu is back in office, the United Nations December 1st, 2022, has called for an Israeli and Palestinian peace summit to be held in, of all places, Moscow, Russia. This doesn't make any sense at all. They are not having a peace summit concerning the Russia/Ukraine war that is currently taking place but yet for the Israel/Palestinian conflict in the capital city of Russia, which has committed so many war crimes. This resolution was approved  154-9, and this peace summit will occur sometime early in 2023—a real head-scratcher.

Emmanuel Macron appears to be playing his role behind the scenes in the shadows right now. Emmanuel Macron was also the European leader who took the helm in holding talks with Vladimir Putin, the leader of the Russian Bear, before and during the Ukraine war in attempts to de-escalate it. Everyone says Macron failed at those negotiations. Did he really? The Bible says that the Bear will be a part of the final beast kingdom. Could Emmanuel Macron be the master puppeteer setting this world up for the collapse in order to take control of it later? We have no clue what Macron and Putin were discussing or planning behind closed doors. Yes, I know these are some bold claims, and we haven't even gotten to the Biblical Characteristics yet.

Before we get into all the Biblical characteristics and attributes connected to Emmanuel Macron, President of France, we will first look at his personal life and how he rose to power out of nowhere to become the President of France.

THE BIO: Rise To Political Power

Emmanuel Jean-Michel Frédéric Macron (born December 21, 1977, in Amiens, France) a French banker and politician elected president of France and the co-prince of Andorra since 2017. Macron was the first person in the history of the Fifth Republic to be elected president without the support of socialists or Gaullists. He is the youngest French head of state since Napoleon I. He was re-elected in 2022, becoming the first French president in two decades to win a second term.

Macron was the oldest of three siblings born to a family of doctors who held politically liberal views. Emmanuel Macron married Brigitte Trogneux in 2007. Brigitte, a former teacher at La Providence high school in Amiens, is 24 years older than him and was married when Macron met her. She had three children from a previous marriage; Macron has no children from his marriage with Brigitte. Brigitte's role in Macron's 2017 presidential campaign has been called pivotal. Macron has three step-children named Sébastien Auzière, an engineer, Laurence Auzière-Jourdan, a cardiologist, and Tiphaine Auzière, a lawyer.

What is Emmanuel Macron's **religion**? He is now an agnostic. Although, at age 12, Macron became baptized as a Catholic at his own request despite growing up in a non-religious family.

In 2001, Macron obtained a master's degree in public policy from Sciences Po and a master's degree in philosophy from the University of Paris Nanterre. In 2004, he graduated with honors from the prestigious Ecole National School of Administration (ENA). This school had a reputation as a quick route to political power.

ANTICHRIST UNMASKED

French presidents Valéry Giscard d'Estaing, Jacques Chirac and François Hollande are all ENA alumni.

Macron was groomed by a global organization called the "World Economic Forum." He was groomed as a "Global Young Leader." What does that mean? The World Economic Forum has been in operation since 1993, a program called *"Global Leaders of Tomorrow,"* rebranded, in 2004, as "Young Global Leaders." This program aims to identify, select, and promote future global leaders in business and politics. Indeed, quite a few "Young Global Leaders" have later managed to become Presidents, Prime Ministers, or CEOs. World Economic Forum founder Klaus Schwab has openly bragged about his organization's ability to infiltrate governments across the world through his program of Young Global Leaders. His organization has groomed leaders such as Emmanuel Macron, Justin Trudeau of Canada, CEO Mark Zuckerberg of Facebook, Pete Buttigieg, US Secretary of Transportation, etc. Earlier members elected in 1992 under its former name of "Global Leaders of Tomorrow" were global profiles such as Angela Merkel of Germany, Tony Blair, Nicolas Sarkozy, Bill Gates, Bono, and many more.

In August 2007, Macron was appointed deputy rapporteur of the "Committee for the Liberation of French Development" by Jacques Attali in order to release French Growth." In 2008, Macron paid €50,000 to get himself out of his contract with the government. In September 2008, Macron left his position as Financial Inspector and took a job at **Rothschild & Cie Banque**. He later received a well-paid position at Rothschild & Cie Banque as an investment banker. His first obligation at Rothschild & Cie Banque was to

ANTICHRIST UNMASKED

assist Crédit Mutuel Nord Europe in the acquisition of Cofidis.

Macron established a relationship with Alain Minc, a businessman and member of the supervisory board of Le Monde. In 2010, Macron was promoted to the bank's partner following the recapitalization of Le Monde and the acquisition of SiemensIT Services and Solutions. That same year, Macron was appointed chief executive officer and was in charge of Nestle's acquisition of one of Pfizer's most significant children's beverage subsidiaries. His share of the €9 billion deal made Macron a millionaire.

Macron reported earnings of €2 million between December 2010 and May 2012. Official documents show that between 2009 and 2013, Macron earned almost €3 million. He left Rothschild & Cie in 2012.

After Hollande won the presidency in 2012, Macron joined his administration as deputy chief of staff and economic adviser. Macron became the face of France at international summits, and in 2014 he was elevated to finance minister. Hollande's approval rating plummeted due to France's anemic economic performance and Europe's ongoing migrant crisis; these factors would fuel the rise of Marine Le Pen and her nationalist anti-immigrant party, the National Front. Macron began to distance himself from Hollande.

In April 2016, Macron declared the creation of his own political party, En Marche! ("Forward!"), a grassroots movement he called a "democratic revolution" against a sclerotic political system. Mirroring the third-way model promoted by President Bill Clinton, Pres. Barack Obama in the United States, and Prime Minister Tony Blair of the UK, Macron proposed a center-left combination of populism and neoliberalism. Observers noted that the announcement's timing - just over a year before the 2017 presidential election - strongly hinted at an outside bid for the Élysée Palace. On August 30, 2016, Macron presented his resignation while keeping his distance from Hollande. On November 16, he officially announced his candidacy for president. Hollande, seeing no practical path to a second term, declared in December 2016 that he would not run for election.

Weak support for France's two main parties opened the door for independent candidates. The race practically became a three-way competition between Macron, Le Pen, and Jean-Luc Mélenchon, a former socialist who ran for president in 2012 with the backing of the Communist Party of France.

In the second round of voting, held on May 7, 2017, Macron won a compelling two-thirds of the vote 66.06%, becoming, at age 39, France's youngest president. Macron assumed office on May 14, 2017, coincidentally Israel's 69th anniversary as a reborn nation. In the June 2017 legislative elections, the new En Marche! The party won a convincing victory, winning 308 out of 577 seats in the National Assembly. With further support from Francois Bayrou's Movement for Democracy (MoDem), Macron's coalition won a total of 350 seats. While the result marked an excellent performance for a party only 14 months old, the turnout was just 42.6%. This was the lowest turnout in a parliamentary election in modern French history. Macron quickly entered the international scene.

THE LIST

As we continue to learn more about Emmanuel Macron, this will be a good point to begin unmasking the Biblical characteristics and attributes associated with Macron as the final Antichrist the Bible speaks of. Here we go!

1)   The Antichrist will be a man.

*Then **he** shall confirm a covenant with many for one week;*
But in the middle of the week
***He** shall bring an end to sacrifice and offering.*
And on the wing of abominations shall be one who makes
desolate, Even until the consummation, which is
determined, Is poured out on the desolate.
Daniel 9:27 NKJV

*The ten horns are **ten kings***
Who shall arise from this kingdom.
And another shall rise after them;
***He** shall be different from the first ones,*
And shall subdue three kings.
*25**He** shall speak pompous words against the Most High,*
Shall persecute the Saints of the Most High,
And shall intend to change times and law.
*Then the Saints shall be given into **his** hand*
For a time and times and half a time. Daniel 7:24-25

*...Whos look was more stout than **his** fellows*
Daniel 7:20 NKJV

*...A **King** of fierce countenance Daniel 8:23 NKJV*

Many other passages indicate that Antichrist is a male ruler of a nation. The Antichrist will be confirming a false covenant with many. He will sit in the newly rebuilt temple, proclaiming himself a god. When this happens, the Bible refers to this action as the abomination of desolation. The Antichrist is not a system or technology like the internet or AI, as some have un-biblically speculated. The Antichrist will be using technology and AI to try to copycat his version of omnipresence that only God possesses; however Antichrist himself will be a male ruler, as the Bible indicates over and over again. We know Emmanuel Macron fits this attribute of being a male ruler of a nation. Pretty easy one here.

2) Let's really begin by looking at his full name and what it means: **Emmanuel Jean-Michel Frédéric Macron.** You must understand that Satan is the father of lies and is very deceptive. So it would make sense that the Antichrist name would be significant as copycatting the name above all names, which is only Jesus the Christ.

*Behold, a virgin shall be with child, and shall bring forth a son, And they shall call his name **Emmanuel**, which being interpreted is, **God with us**.*
Matthew 1:23 KJV

Emmanuel - God with us
Jean - God is gracious or gift from God
Michel - French for "Michael" meaning: who is like God?
Frédéric - peaceful ruler (Prince of Peace is the title for Jesus Christ)
Macron - a short, straight **mark** <u>placed</u> over a vowel. (The Antichrist will require people to take his mark in order to be able to buy or sell <u>placed</u> on your right hand or forehead known as the mark of the beast)

Considering the fact that Macron's parents are non-religious, it seems a bit strange that they would name their child in this way.

Take a look at Emmanuel Macron's signature. The way he signs his name is very narcissistic, arrogant, and diabolical. Attributes we will expound on later.

Signature

Do you see what I see? You see his last name, Macron, without the "m." Instead of signing his first name Emmanuel, he replaces his first name with the symbol of a shepherd's staff that intersects at the bottom with a snake-like zig zag to form an upside-down cross. Also, note that the shepherd's staff also forms the number seven. This is God's number of perfection. In Macron's signature, he is blaspheming the cross of Christ while trying to say he is above Jesus, who is the true God (1 John 5:20). There is no other reason why he signs his name the way he does. It doesn't look like an "m," nor does it look like the word Emmanuel. It's intensional symbolism.

Here's a bonus: another strange observation that I'm not even considering in my official list is Macron's birthday. He was born on December 21st, 1977, during the Winter Solstice, the shortest day of the year. One reason speculated why December 25th was picked for Jesus' birthday is because it was considered to be during the Winter Solstice or the shortest day of the year.

3)   The number 666 will be associated with the Antichrist in many ways, and his name can also, be calculated to the number 666.

*And I saw something like a sea of glass mingled with fire, and those who have the victory over the beast, over his image and over his mark and over the **number of his name**...Revelation 15:2 NKJV*

*Here is wisdom. Let him who has understanding **calculate the number of the beast**, for it is the **number of a man**: His number is **666**. Revelation 13:18 NKJV*

2017

There are 36 (**6 x 6**) total characters in Macron's name (32 letters, one dash, three spaces).

Emmanuel Jean-Michel Frédéric Macron = 666

If you give each character a value of its position and calculate the sum, you get **666** (1+2+3+... +36 = 666).

4) The Antichrist will claim to be god.

Let no one deceive you by any means; for that Day will not come unless the falling away comes first, and the man of sin is revealed, the son of perdition, 4who opposes and **exalts himself above all that is called God** *or that is worshiped, so that he sits as God in the temple of God,* **showing himself that he is God***.*
2 Thessalonians 2:3-4 NKJV

We have already seen from Macron's signature through symbolism, he makes the statement of exalting himself above God every time he signs his name. Emmanuel Macron also arrogantly proclaimed from his mouth at the beginning of his presidency that he would rule like the Roman god Jupiter. The highest-ranked pagan god in the Roman and Greek pantheons. When the media asked officials of the Elysée Palace for a QA afterward, they responded that the 39-year old's thoughts were "too complex" for journalists.

Macron walked out to the European Union's national anthem, "Ode to Joy," a song about god, instead of the French national anthem when he made his presidential victory speech.

Video

Macron's nickname in France today is "Jupiter." Additional names given to him include: "Jesus Macron," "Savior of Europe," and "new Louis XIV" (or the resurrected "Sun King"). Folks, you can't make this stuff up.

ANTICHRIST UNMASKED

5)   The Antichrist will be a Prince.

And after the sixty-two weeks
Messiah shall be cut off, but not for Himself;
*And the people of **the <u>prince</u> who is to come***
Shall destroy the city and the sanctuary.
The end of it shall be with a flood,
And till the end of the war desolations are determined.
Daniel 9:26 NKJV

Did you know Satan himself also holds the title of a prince? As a matter of fact, many in the angelic heavenly realms have titles or a hierarchy of princes. Michael the Archangel is considered the "great Prince or Chief Prince" Daniel 12:1, Daniel 10:13. Satan, also an angel is the "prince of the power of the air."

Why am I mentioning this, you ask? Satan, along with the angels that follow him, will be cast down to earth after the battle (Revelation 12:7-12) that takes place in heaven against Michael and his angels. Satan will no longer have the ability to go back and forth through the heavenly realms. This battle will take place at the 3 1/2 year mark of the final seven years, at the time of the abomination of desolation. Satan will know his time is short, and the Antichrist at this time will be possessed by the "prince of the power of the air," Satan.

So see, the Antichrist may very well be an earthly prince; however, he will most certainly be a spiritually evil prince. Is there a parallel right now that can be associated with the President of France, Emmanuel Macron?

Unlike most European and western leaders, Macron is a prince. Emmanuel Macron became co-prince of Andorra, a tiny principality between France and Spain, at the same time he took office. The title of Co-Prince of Andorra is an automatic perk given to the Head of State of France. It all dates back to an agreement signed in 1278 when the bishop and Count of Foix agreed to avoid war by identifying themselves as co-princes.

6) The Antichrist will not regard the desire of women.

*He shall regard neither the God of his fathers **nor the desire of women**...Daniel 11:37 NKJV*

I will repeat. Some interpretations are that this must mean Antichrist has to be gay. Also, another understanding that I lean more towards is that this would mean the Antichrist would not have any children of his own. After all, what do most women desire? Children. So the Antichrist, not regarding the desire of women, would mean no children of his own. I wouldn't expect Antichrist to share his glory with offspring, so this seems to make more sense. Also, Antichrist being a cheap copycat; Jesus didn't have any children. If you remember reading in Macron's bio, though he has stepchildren from his wife's previous marriage, Macron himself has no children of his own. This puts Macron in a very elite category regarding this particular characteristic.

7) As we have already learned from the "Antichrist" chapter, he and the False Prophet will come from Europe.

*8I was considering the **horns**, and there was another horn, a **little one, coming up among them**, before whom three of the first horns were plucked out by the roots. And there, **in this horn, were eyes like the eyes of a man, and a mouth speaking pompous words**. Daniel 7:8 NKJV*

The Antichrist will arise out of a ten-kingdom alliance. We know that the ten horns represent ten nations and the leaders of these nations. This will constitute the Holy Roman Empire.

France is a powerful country located in Europe. Angela Merkel, the former Chancellor of Germany, stepped down in 2021 and was considered the leader of the European Union. France and Germany have always had a close relationship and formed the Franco-German Alliance after WW2, which led them to create the European Union.

It appears that Merkel's void is being filled now by Emmanuel Macron as the de facto leader of the European Union. Again he is the one that held talks with Putin on behalf of Europe. Macron is the one that all newly elected leaders worldwide are flocking to first.

In the first chapter of the book, we talk about the four beasts of Daniel chapter 7 and how they are mentioned again in Revelation chapter 13 as a cohesive combo beast representing the Antichrist's final Kingdom. We discussed how the eagle's wings (U.S.) are not mentioned in chapter 13 but are found in Revelation chapter 12:14 protecting Israel and therefore are not a part of the beast kingdom of chapter 13. Surprisingly another observation found in Daniel chapter 7 that we learned was that the Leopard (Germany) had wings of a fowl (France). We learned that this represented the German & Franco Alliance. In Revelation chapter 13, you find the leopard again, but like the eagle's wings, you don't see the wings of the fowl that were associated with the leopard. The question is, what happened to the fowl wings or France? The Bible does not mention the fowl wings again in relation to the four beasts. This observation is very intriguing.

Could the little horn, who we know is the Antichrist, be the reason we don't find the fowl wings mentioned in Revelation chapter 13, or anywhere? There will be no longer just a German / Franco alliance, but Emmanuel Macron of France as the little horn leading the entire global beast system alliance for 42 months, the last 3.5 years of Daniel's 70th week.

The fact that the fowl wings (France) of Daniel chapter 7 are never mentioned again speaks volumes that they are being re-represented as the nation or horn the Antichrist will be coming from. This points to the country of France, whose President currently is Emmanuel Macron.

8)   The Antichrist will be very dark and
       sinister.

"And in the latter time of their kingdom,
When the transgressors have reached their fullness,
A king shall arise,
*Having **fierce features,***
***Who understands sinister schemes**. Daniel 8:23 NKJV*

Though I believe this passage primarily refers to the 3 1/2 year point of the final seven years when the Antichrist commits the abomination of desolation and is possessed by Satan himself and then given authority to rule for the remaining 42 months. Emmanuel Macron has already shown some of these attributes. During Trump's first Whitehouse visit by a statesman, Macron Video exhibited some of his darkness in late April 2018. Macron deliberately flashes the satanic symbol of the devil horns while standing next to Trump on the Whitehouse's balcony facing the crowds and the cameras. You can see in the video Trump tries to pull Macron's hand down, but that didn't stop Macron from continuing to

flash those horns outwardly toward America. When watching the video, also pay attention to Macron's facial expression. He knows exactly what he is doing and is brazen in not hiding who he represents.

What does this satanic hand gesture mean? **Horned Hand** – The sign of recognition between those in the Occult. When pointed at someone, it is intended to place a curse on them.

Two years after Macron's visit, the Pandemic began, resulting in changes in how the U.S. cast votes that opened the door to widespread voting fraud. Trump lost his re-election bid after receiving more votes than any sitting president in history.

Trump and Macron were constantly at odds with one another. Trump, as an anti-globalist, pulled America out of many of the global entities and funding provided. While Macron has been and still is the most prominent spokesman for globalism and climate change initiatives that change laws that control and affect how people live their lives, all in the name of the "greater good."

What Macron exhibited at the Whitehouse with his hand-horned gesture late April 2018 was sinister.

sinister
<u>adjective</u>
a. *Suggesting or threatening harm or evil.*
b. *Causing or intending harm or evil; wicked.*
c. *Portending misfortune or disaster; ominous.*

Macron always has and still does exhibit darkness through his speech and actions. I'm confident the private talks Macron has had with Putin before, and during the Ukraine invasion were sinister and scheming. Again this may sound bold to say such things, but this is the kind of person the Antichrist will be. We also know that the Bear will be a part of his final beast kingdom. The Antichrist does not care for humanity one bit. Humanity represents the image of God. Satan will try to eliminate humanity through death or by the lie of the mark of the beast. He is trying to prevent Jesus's second coming. If no one is available to be raptured, then Satan believes he wins therefore controlling the world unabated. This is the connection to the Days of Noah. During the days of Noah, Nephilim filled the earth by means of sexual relations between fallen angels and human women (Genesis 6:4). Satan was trying to prevent Jesus's first coming, who he knew would come through the bloodline of the seed of a woman (Genesis 3:15). Satan was trying to taint this bloodline. The Mark of the Beast will ever so slightly change the human DNA code. At the same time, anyone who doesn't take the mark Satan will try to eliminate by killing them, leaving no one to be raptured. Until then Antichrist who now hides in the shadows, and those in the hierarchy of globalism have no

concern if swaths of humanity are killed off prior to his global authority. This is why you see a war that appears to be nuclear mentioned in Revelation chapter 9 that kills 1/3 of humankind before Antichrist revealing. God will allow Antichrist to use sinister schemes for a time.

9) The Antichrist will rule a ten nation confederacy.

*"The **ten horns** which you saw are **ten kings** who have received no kingdom as yet, but **they receive authority for one hour as kings with the beast.** 13These are of one mind, and **they will give their power and authority to the beast.** Revelation 17:12-13 NKJV*

Emmanuel Macron since 2018 has been working on building a ten-nation European Army to reduce reliance on the United States. He continues to cultivate it to this day. Ten nations did agree to an alliance back in June of 2018.

Here's an excerpt from a UK newspaper called "The Week." It even lists ten nations who signed on to this coalition. We will not know whether these are the final ten nations mentioned in the Bible until the final 3 1/2 years of the Great Tribulation. Power will be given over to the Antichrist to rule over these ten nations.

*"A coalition of ten European militaries ready to defend the continent's borders has been unveiled in Paris, just days after **Emmanuel Macron called for a "real European army."***

*"Finland has joined Germany, Belgium, Britain, Denmark, Estonia, the Netherlands, Spain, and Portugal in the **French-led initiative**, which will see members collaborate on planning, on the analysis of new military and humanitarian crises, and on eventual military responses to those crises."*
The Week, UK, June 2018

The ten-nation alliance mentioned in Revelation are the nations that the Antichrist will lead during the Battle of Armageddon to come against **Jesus and all of the Saints** who were just raptured prior to this battle. It appears from scripture that this Antichrist kingdom that consists of a ten-nation army will not be compelled to give up their full authority until the end. It will take some time for this coalition of nations to develop into a strong army. Something to consider is that at the time of the "abomination of desolation" after the war in heaven against Michael the Archangel, the angels that follow after Satan will also be cast down to earth. I'm confident they will be added to the army of the Antichrist. Allowing the Antichrist army to be exceedingly stronger than any other on the planet.

Though at the time of the writing of this book, the final seven years have not begun yet, Emmanuel Macron has already started and will continue to cultivate this last day's kingdom and army.

These will make war with the Lamb, and the Lamb will overcome them, for He is Lord of lords and King of kings; and those who are with Him are called, chosen, and faithful." Revelation 17:14 NKJV

10) The Antichrist shall use great military might to forge his authority throughout the world.

And arms shall stand on his part, and they shall pollute the sanctuary of strength, and shall take away the daily sacrifice, and they shall place the abomination that maketh desolate. Daniel 11:31 KJV

This attribute piggybacks off the last one we just mentioned. The Antichrist will use military force to try to force all into conformity into his new world order. The Antichrist will have the backing of the ten-nation coalition that will be the buckle of his strength, the entire United Nations, and the fallen angels.

As we can see from Daniel, the Antichrist will use military force to stop the sacrifices and commit the abomination of desolation. This will be when some Jews realize that the man who helped forge the false covenant 3 1/2 years prior may not be who they thought he was. It will be after the abomination of desolation that we will see the 144,000 and the two witnesses come onto the scene.

Presently France is considered the number 1 military by strength in the 26-nation European Union and boasts as the 7th strongest military in the entire world. The UK of Great Britain (Lion) and France are the only ones that hold nuclear arsenals in the European Union.

I discovered something else to consider through my studies: the "guillotine" was introduced into France in 1792.

 *"During the French Revolution, the guillotine became the **primary symbol of the Reign of Terror** and was used to execute thousands of people, including King Louis XVI and Marie-Antoinette."* britannica.com

You may be asking why am I mentioning this? The guillotine may be brought back as the weapon of choice used by the Antichrist to kill the multitude of martyrs during the Great Tribulation. It has a direct historical connection to France.

*And I saw thrones, and they sat on them, and judgment was committed to them. Then I saw the **souls of those who had been beheaded** for their witness to Jesus and for the word of God, who had not worshiped the beast or his image, and had not received his mark on their foreheads or on their hands... Revelation 20:4 NKJV*

11) The Antichrist will be very haughty, proud, and arrogant. He will be a psychopathic narcissist.

"Through his cunning
He shall cause deceit to prosper under his rule;
***And he shall exalt himself in his heart**.*
Daniel 8:25 NKJV

*"Then the king shall do according to his own will: **he shall exalt and magnify himself** above every god...*
Daniel 11:36 NKJV

We learned from attribute #4 that Emmanuel Macron has already stated that he planned to rule like the Roman god Jupiter. By making a statement like this, Macron is, in essence, already magnifying himself above every god. Jupiter was considered the king of gods in Ancient Roman Mythology. Jupiter is the top god of the Roman pantheon.

Macron's arrogance has been on display many times. Remember, right out of the gates after being elected; he did not participate in the traditional French Presidents' Bastille Day TV interview. The reason given was that Macron's thought process might prove to be "too complex" for journalists. After this stunt of skipping out on this interview, critics portrayed him as "arrogant."

12) The Antichrist will be worshiped through a one world religion.

All who dwell on the earth will worship him, whose names have not been written in the Book of Life of the Lamb slain from the foundation of the world. Revelation 13:8 NKJV

As we have already learned, whoever the Pope is during Daniel's seventh week and when the Antichrist is revealed globally at the 3 1/2 year point is who will be the False Prophet. We also learned that the 1st Seal White horse is represented by not a person but an entity. That entity is Catholicism. The False Prophet will be one of the primary figureheads pointing people to the Antichrist as he rises to power in the first 3 1/2 years. The False Prophet will demand all to worship the Antichrist during the remaining 3 1/2 years through this global one-world religion.

If the Antichrist is hiding in the shadows, presently, one would think he would have to already have a connection to Catholicism as well as a unique relationship with the figurehead of the office of the Pope right now. This relationship will have begun to be forged before the final seven years in order for the figurehead of the office of the Pope (False Prophet) to be so adamant in pointing people to the Antichrist as who their supreme leader should be. Does Emmanuel Macron have such a connection and unique, rare relationship with the Pope and Catholicism?

As we have already learned from Macron's Bio, at age 12, Macron became baptized as a Catholic at his request despite growing up in a non-religious family. Though Macron now considers himself agnostic, the connection between himself and Catholicism was made at a young age under peculiar circumstances, to say the least. I can't help but be reminded that at the age of 12, Jesus was found by Mary and Joseph sitting in the temple among teachers who were astonished by him. This is the age that Jesus began to grow in wisdom and stature among men and in favor with God (Luke 2:42-52). Satan's son, so to speak, is nothing more than a cheap evil counterfeit trying to mimic attributes that Jesus carried when he was here the first time.

Macron visited the Vatican in 2018. The Pope bestowed upon the French President the "First And Only Honorary Canon Of The Archbasilica Of St. John Lateran." The Archbasilica of Saint John Lateran is the seat of the Pope - the bishop of Rome. It is the highest-ranked cathedral in all of Catholicism.

For centuries the Catholic Church has held a special place for the country of France, which has been noted as "*the Church's eldest daughter.*" Several of Macron's predecessors have declined the title, including the Socialists François Mitterrand and François Hollande, a self-described atheist, to avoid associating themselves with religious imagery. France is known as a secular country with a strict separation between Church and state. For Macron to receive this honor was significant, considering France's strict separation of Church and state. After being elected, President Macron did not hesitate and immediately accepted this honor. A Catholic news correspondent posed the question, "Has the eldest daughter of the Church returned?"

Video

Macron's visit with the Pope in 2018 was twice as long as any statesmen prior and ended with an odd kiss by Macron on both cheeks of the Pope. Though some French greet one another with a kiss. No one kisses the Pope. There have been those that have kissed the Pope's ring. You may also see someone shake his hand or give a slight bow but not grab the Pope and kiss him.

13) Antichrist will honor the god of fortresses.

*But in their place **he shall honor a god of fortresses**; and <u>a god which his fathers did not know</u> he shall honor with gold and silver, with precious stones and pleasant things. Daniel 11:38 NKJV*

Many scholars and pastors have been somewhat baffled by the term "god of fortresses" and its meaning. You wouldn't think Antichrist would honor any other god. Let's see if we can figure this one out.

First, it appears this passage refers to two gods, not just one! The word "and" grammatically means "addition too." The second part is what throws a lot of scholars off a bit.

One clue given to us in this passage; it will be a god that no one knows. It will be a brand new god or religion. This god will not come from any religion represented today. I know what you're thinking; I thought whoever the Pope at the current time would be the false prophet, so wouldn't the one world religion be Catholicism? Yes, the Pope will be the "False Prophet" propping up the Antichrist instead of Jesus Christ; however, the False Prophet will be creating a new world religion dedicated to worshiping only the Antichrist and no other gods. *"a god which his fathers did not know"* means Antichrist will essentially be worshiping Satan through himself. Remember, the Antichrist will be possessed by Satan himself at the abomination of desolation. The Antichrist will be the exact opposite of Jesus. Jesus proclaimed He is the only way to the father and is himself the True God. Essentially *"a god which his fathers did not know"* is Satan incarnate through the Antichrist in the flesh. Antichrist will, in fact, be a new god in the world, representing not the Truth who is Jesus but instead the Lie who is Satan.

ANTICHRIST UNMASKED

We are already seeing the collaboration of faiths and religions today through "inter-faithism," which is currently being heavily promoted by the Pope to bring all religions together under one umbrella as reaching god through many paths. This new religion is under development today for the future purpose of worshiping this new god who will proclaim to be above every god, demanding all to worship him. The people and religions of the world are being programmed for this now. Let me remind you what Jesus stated; "I am the Truth and the way, and the life" in other words, Jesus is it. Jesus proclaimed himself as the only exclusive way. There is no other name under heaven by which a person can be saved (Acts 4:12). In the end, there will be only two options, not a 1,000 different religions or gods to choose from. The clutter of religion will be removed, leaving those alive during the last days with a clear choice. God will make it really simple for those of us living during the end, choose Antichrist or choose Jesus Christ.

So as we have just established, this new god will be the Antichrist worshiping Satan through himself. What about the first part, *"he shall honor the god of fortresses"*? Daniel chapter 11 is about military forces coming against other military forces. This statement is in direct relation to military and military defense. The passage also states Antichrist will honor it with gold and silver etc. This means he will direct most of his kingdom's finances to military and warfare. The Antichrist will try to conquer and control the world through military force. He will do everything primarily through the military, just like in the old Roman era. For example, we learned in attribute #10 that Antichrist would use military force to take over the temple.

This is a future attribute; however, coincidentally, as we already have learned, Emmanuel Macron has claimed he wants to rule **like** the god of Jupiter. According to Greek mythology, one of Jupiter's primary characteristics is that he was the "god of war," which is the same as "the god of fortresses" that Daniel talks about in chapter 11. Macron has also stated that he wants his government to be a Jupiterian-style government. Let's not forget the ten-nation European army that Macron is forging as Europe's defense force so as not to rely on other countries such as the United States. This man's heart, from the beginning, has been compelled toward the "god of fortresses."

Folks, we are at number 13 on our list. We are past the probability of coincidences here. So far, everything has pointed to Emmanuel Macron and or France. We still have a few more to cover, and it's about to get even more incredible and jolting.

14) The Antichrist will have strong ties with ancient Assyria.

*Therefore thus says the Lord God of hosts: "O My people, who dwell in Zion, do not be afraid of the **Assyrian**. He shall strike you with a rod and lift up his staff against you... Isaiah 10:24 NKJV*

Because of this attribute, there are those who believe that it proves Antichrist will have to come from the middle east. Does it really? There are many other passages we have already taken a look at that point to Antichrist coming from Europe. The new Holy Roman Empire. Which is it? Is this a contradiction?

One type of Antichrist figure from Bible history was Antiochus Epiphanes, a Greek King of the Seleucid Empire who reigned over Syria from 175BC - 164BC. "Epiphanes" means "god manifest." Antiochus Epiphanes was such a

ANTICHRIST UNMASKED

tyrannical figure that some today believe he was the last days' Antichrist. Antiochus erected an altar to Zeus/Jupiter on top of the altar of burnt offerings and sacrificed a pig. These acts were considered an abomination of desolation to the 1st Jewish Temple. Antiochus Epiphanes is very domineering in Jewish history and foreshadows the coming Antichrist; however, with over 50 Biblical characteristics, it's easier to disqualify someone than to qualify them. Daniel chapter 11 parallels Antiochus Epiphanes to the last days' Antichrist. A definitive transition between them both happens in Daniel 11:36, which states, *"he will prosper until the wrath has been accomplished."* This passage means the Antichrist will prosper until God's wrath is completed (the 7 bowls).

Antiochus Epiphanes has been dead for well over 2,000 years. We know from Revelation chapter 16 that the wrath of God doesn't begin until the mark of the beast is administered. The 1st bowl of God's wrath is doled out on those that take the mark. Though we are getting very close, we aren't living under such a global system yet. We know that Jesus throws the Antichrist and False Prophet into the lake of fire following the Great battle of Armageddon. Human government is removed, and the "ancient of days" (Jesus) is immediately transitioned to rule and reign for the following 1,000 years and forevermore. These events are still yet to happen while Antiochus Epiphanes is lying in his grave currently. All of this and more disqualifies Antiochus Epiphanes as the last days' Antichrist.

So, where am I going with all of this, and how does Emmanuel Macron fit in? Would it shock you to find out that there is a strange connection and possible ancestry relationship between Antiochus Epiphanes's top general and Emmanuel Macron?

We already know Macron's strange ties to Catholicism from a young age, so it shouldn't be a surprise that through the Catholic historical records, we would discover yet another strange coincidence that Emmanuel Macron has with Antiochus Epiphanes. You see, the Roman Catholic Apocrypha, which is not to be confused with the Holy Bible, has some additional historical data as it relates to Antiochus Epiphanes. It's found in the book Maccabees that the Roman Catholic Church accepts. I want to clarify that I'm not espousing the Apocrypha or the book of Maccabees at all as authoritative. It wasn't allowed into the final canon of the Holy Bible that God divinely inspired as His word to the world. The main point I'm trying to make is that there is a connection between Emmanuel Macron and Antiochus Epiphanes that strangely can only be found through Roman Catholic history. There was a general of King Antiochus of Syria named Ptolemy Dorymenes, who was given the cognomen, or third name of MACRON. Ptolemy Macron was an enemy of the Jewish People. King Antiochus Epiphanes sent Ptolemy Macron to fight against the Jews under the Maccabees. Have your eyebrows risen?

Let me continue to remind you what Emmanuel Macron stated early in his presidency from his own mouth that he would rule like the Roman god "Jupiter." The same god that Antiochus Epiphanes used to desecrate the 1st Jewish temple. We now know that "Macron" was a Roman-appointed surname to a top general of Antiochus Epiphanes who hated the Jews. You can't make this stuff up, people! I've ensured that everything I'm presenting to you is verifiable because I knew such claims would sound bazaar. My mouth dropped when I first found this out myself. I'm not saying there is a direct ancestry

ANTICHRIST UNMASKED

line here; there could be. What I am saying is that the parallels that can be made between the current President of France, Emmanuel Macron, and the Assyrian empire are without question. That's a fact.

The plot thickens. Does the country of France have any ties to the land that once was Ancient Assyria? Well, they do. In 1920, soon after the end of World War I, the League of Nations mandated that Lebanon would be administered by France after the Partition of the Ottoman Empire. Lebanon officially became part of the French colonial empire as part of the French Mandate for Syria and Lebanon and was administered from Damascus. In January 1944, France agreed to transfer power to the Lebanese government, thus granting the territory independence.

The land known as Lebanon today was a part of the Ancient Assyrian Empire that later France controlled for a time hence their colonial ties to this middle eastern Assyrian land. The official language today in Lebanon is Arabic, while French is also formally recognized.

Back in 2020, when Lebanon had a massive explosion in its capital city Beirut, Macron was there just days following to lend support and aid to this country, even to the extent of helping them form a new government. When Macron arrived, he planted a cedar tree in acknowledgment of the history and support that France and Lebanon share. This man is driven by symbolism. Let's take a look at Ezekiel 31.

1And it came to pass in the eleventh year, in the third month, in the first day of the month, that the word of the LORD came unto me, saying, 2Son of man, speak unto Pharaoh king of Egypt, and to his multitude; Whom art thou like in thy greatness? ***3Behold, the Assyrian was a cedar in Lebanon*** *with fair branches, and with a shadowing shroud, and of an high stature; and his top was among the thick boughs. Ezekiel 31:1-3 KJV*

The prophet Ezekiel often referenced a person called the Assyrian, who is an Old Testament reference to the future Antichrist; here, he is compared to a tree in Lebanon just before the start of the time of Jacob's trouble (mid-point of final seven years). Emmanuel Macron was in Lebanon planning how to create a new government there. Macron planted a cedar tree acknowledging their shared historical ties just before he began to advise them.

After reviewing Biblical, historical and current events, my question to you is; do you think there could be more than a distinct possibility that France's President Emmanuel Macron could be the Assyrian mentioned in the Bible? I do, and the question of whether there is a contradiction if the Antichrist will come from the middle east or Europe Emmanuel Macron solves.

15)   The Antichrist will confirm a covenant that last seven years.

Then **he shall confirm a covenant with many for one week**;*But in the middle of the week*
He shall bring an end to sacrifice and offering.
And on the wing of abominations shall be one who makes desolate, Even until the consummation, which is determined, Is poured out on the desolate."
Daniel 9:27 NKJV

You need to understand a few keywords from this passage so that you will see the gravity of what is meant and how they presently connect to only Emmanuel Macron. The "**he**" here is the Antichrist. The Antichrist will be **confirming** (*To strengthen or make stronger*) a covenant between Israel and **many** other nations, including the Palestinian people. We discussed this covenant earlier in the Antichrist chapter. The length of this covenant will last "one symbolic week," this is a week of years, not days, with each day representing a year. Also, I would like to add if the Antichrist will be confirming/strengthening a covenant, this would suggest something else would have already been in place at the time of the "confirming."

This attribute hasn't happened yet. When it does happen, this event will launch humankind into the final seven years until Jesus returns for his Church (rapture).

So, how does Emmanuel Macron fit into this attribute of Daniel 9:27? Though this event hasn't happened yet, Emmanuel Macron has already suggested nearly verbatim what Daniel 9:27 mentions. Earlier in May of 2022, on Israel's Independence Day, Emmanuel Macron made some remarks about Israel. I'm going to share with you a couple of his comments. The first has a European connection to Israel, and the second has a Daniel 9:27 connection. These remarks are taken from the "European Jewish Press, EJP."

*"You can count on **me** to strengthen France's ties with Israel at all levels, including the European level." EJP*

This first remark goes along with the Bible that Antichrist will come from the European region. Macron's remark making a direct correlation between France and all of Europe would be something you would expect a European Antichrist figure to say while trying to bring Israel into the fold of his future European plan of peace for Israel that will include "many." The second comment below from Macron confirms his intention, which is taken from Daniel 9:27.

*"I also want to commend the commitment of Israel and our Arab partners who gave birth to the **Abraham Accords**. They contribute to **stability and peace**. They must be **strengthened** and **expanded**," the French President, who was reelected for a second term two weeks ago, added. EJP*

Abraham Accords - would be the "covenant" already in place.

Strengthened and **Expanded** - "Confirm" with "Many"

Following this astonishing statement, Macron goes on to say that this is what must be done to pave the way for Israel and Palestinian sovereignty and security.

I don't know how many more Jaw dropping proofs I can provide you, but this is unreal. What are the odds that what Macron is saying literally comes straight from a passage of scripture that references the Antichrist as who will be making such a covenant in the way the Bible describes that begins the final seven years? Only the man of sin would make such comments like this. It's predetermined in his heart. Was Macron sowing the seed and foreshadowing what is to come? Time will tell. It doesn't seem like we will be waiting too long for the answer on this one.

16)   He will be preceded by 7 kings he himself will be the 8th.

10There are also seven kings. Five have fallen, one is, and the other has not yet come. And when he comes, he must continue a short time. 11The beast that was, and is not, is himself also the eighth, and is of the seven, and is going to perdition. Revelation 17:10-11 NKJV

Out of all the characteristics the Bible provides about the Antichrist, it's this one right here that points directly to the actual individual himself. This passage gives us clues as to which nation the Antichrist will be coming from and which king he will be. When Identifying these two key components, you will know who the actual person is.

The traditional belief is that this passage refers to past kingdoms or empires (Egypt, Assyria, Babylon, Medo-Persia, Greece, Rome, and the final kingdom of the Antichrist). There are a couple of problems with this line of thinking. First of all, this passage is referencing Kings, not Kingdoms. In the list, they assume there are seven final kingdoms. However, if I entertained this line of thought, it still doesn't make sense. We were already told in Daniel that there would be only five kingdoms, and it's the fifth and final kingdom that Antichrist rises from, not a seventh kingdom. We covered this in the Antichrist chapter.

*32This image's **head was of fine gold**, its **chest and arms of silver**, its **belly and thighs of bronze**, 33its **legs of iron**, its **feet partly of iron and partly of clay**. Daniel 2:32-33 NKJV*

Revelation 17:10-11 doesn't state that this references different Kingdoms but Kings (individuals) themselves. Also, this passage says the Antichrist *"is the eighth and is of the seven."* This clearly means all of these kings, including the Antichrist, are from the same kingdom, not seven different kingdoms. We also see following this prophetic fulfillment that destruction follows at some point in the near future ("goeth into perdition").

Let's look at this passage with fresh eyes. One might think it would seem impossible for someone now to fit this prophecy in its "literal" understanding, especially during present circumstances. Would the Antichrist only be the eighth king (leader)? It didn't make sense to me either; after all, at the time of the writing of this book, the United States, for example, has had 46 Presidents in its short 246-year life span. It's been nearly 2000 years since Jesus was here on earth, and for the Antichrist to be only the eighth seemed unrealistic. Not to mention his two predecessors would still be living while the first five kings "fallen" (are dead).

For those of you that have read my book "The EndTime Is Now," I believe quite a few significant events have already taken place; some Seals, Trumpets, etc. This does not mean the final seven years have started; nowhere in

ANTICHRIST UNMASKED

Revelation does it state that all of these events are only confined to the final seven years. I think the Bible describes those events right along with historical events that have already taken place. We are just waiting and watching for a few more to come to pass that eventually ends at the rapture and 2nd coming of Jesus to the earth. To me, the explanations backed with scripture and historical facts to go along with it make for a very compelling case than the allegorical stories great scholars try to use in describing events that they don't know have already happened. I mean, they are pretty far-fetched with their imaginations! If a Bible prophecy has already been fulfilled, you should be able to back it up with all kinds of data, historical facts, pictures, etc. That's what I tried to accomplish when writing my first book. In doing so by default, it also points out the flaws used in traditional Bible prophecy teachings.

I said all that to say; I believe previous interpretations by scholars and pastors of Revelation 17:10-11 are incorrect. This passage, like other prophecies when they were fulfilled, is relevant to our current situation right now as we see this prophecy being fulfilled today. All pieces to this prophetic fulfillment must fit together like a nice neat puzzle. The final piece to this puzzle was laid down and completed on 12/02/2020 to this particular prophecy about the Antichrist. Until December 2020, I haven't found anyone presently or historically that would have been able to meet all the requirements this particular prophecy calls for to be fulfilled. For right now, this prophecy fits perfectly for Emmanuel Macron when it hasn't for anyone else in history at any time. This is why I believe the false peace deal could soon be on the horizon. The window is presently wide open for Emmanuel Macron for a while. It's during this open window the false covenant would have to be made and would fit precisely in accordance with the prophecy mentioned here in Revelation chapter 17 when he goes into perdition and ultimately is possessed by Satan himself at the 3 1/2 year point. According to its literal understanding, I don't see the circumstances of this particular prophecy lining up again for anyone else for ages.

I was intrigued by this attribute because it provides specific detailed requirements in such an orderly fashion. I knew that if we were living in the end times and this person was on earth today; this attribute would have already been fulfilled or close to it. I extensively researched Revelation 17:10-11 to see if anyone historically or presently came close to matching this specific attribute. Long story short, I found that the Country of France was close to completing this prophecy. No other country, past or present, came close. I researched the history of the Rulers of France.

You will see from the link that France has had its government restarted several times throughout history. Currently, France's government structure is under the "Fifth Republic"; presently, Emmanuel Macron is the 8th Leader. The first five are deceased; number 6, Nicolas Sarkozy, and 7, Francois Holland, are still alive and only served a short time, which leads to #8 currently, Emmanuel Macron, serving his 2nd term, the first to do so in over 20 years. He is the 8th leader under France's current government structure. The Bible is, of course, speaking about the time of the Antichrist during his modern era. I say this prophecy was fulfilled on 12/02/2020 because "Valéry Giscard d'Estaing," the 3rd ruler under Frances' current government structure, died on 12/02/2020. He would complete the first five that have fallen. The only part of this prophecy that

ANTICHRIST UNMASKED

hasn't been fulfilled is that the Antichrist has yet to go into perdition. The false covenant would need to happen first. "Going into perdition" directly refers to the 42 months or final 3.5 years of the seven-year period the Antichrist is granted authority. If Emmanuel Macron is the Antichrist, the window for the false peace deal is now opened and could theoretically stay open through 2027, concluding Emmanuel Macron's Presidency of France.

☰ ThoughtCo. 🔍

Fifth Republic (Presidents)

Charles de Gaulle returned to try and calm social unrest and began the Fifth Republic, which still forms the government structure of contemporary France. Revelation 17:10-11

- 1959–1969 Charles de Gaulle · · · 5
- 1969–1974 Georges Pompidou · · · F
- 1974–1981 Valéry Giscard d'Estaing · A
  Died 12/02/2020 · · · L
- 1981–1995 François Mitterand · · · L
- 1995–2007 Jacques Chirac · · · E
  · · · N
- 2007–2012 Nicolas Sarkozy ⎫ Alive
- 2012–2017 Francois Hollande ⎭
- 2017–present Emmanuel Macron   8th

*10There are also seven kings. Five have fallen, one is, and the other has not yet come. And when he comes, he must continue a short time. 11The beast that was, and is not, is himself also the **eighth**, and is of the seven, and is going to perdition. Revelation 17:10-11 NKJV*

Everything is set, and the only thing left for the complete fulfillment of this prophecy is that he goes into perdition. This can only happen at the midpoint of the final seven-year period when Antichrist is granted 42 months of authority. We know that the confirmed covenant of Daniel 9:27 has to happen first. This all means that the launch of the final seven years is closer now than ever before.

I mentioned in my introduction that one of the highlights of this book is that I believed I was going to show you something in the Bible for the "first time" that no one has realized points precisely to one undeniable individual. I hope you are as amazed as I was when I discovered this attribute. The best way to discern Bible prophecy is to try not to overthink or overcomplicate it. This specific Bible prophecy wasn't meant to be understood until all the pieces were in place. Past scholars and pastors were trying to put a square cube into a round hole. Trying to make specific ideas and thoughts fit into this prophecy in order to be able to have an explanation for it when it was not yet time. You see, sometimes you must live through certain things before understanding them. I think  that's why God told Daniel in Daniel 12:8-10 that his visions would be sealed until the time of the end. Daniel's generation was not living through what he was seeing in his visions which made Daniel very perplexed. We, though, are living through what Daniel and John the Revelator both prophesied. Bible prophecy is becoming easier to understand by the day, with all events converging rapidly during our time. All the prophetic dots are connecting. This is a blessing to those who read and understand Bible prophecy, as Revelation 1:3 states. The blessing is that we are able to have the foresight to navigate through these last-day events to be used on the other side of them. This allows us to reach as many to Jesus as we can while we endure until the end.

In closing, we just went through 16 bullet points using 25 passages of scripture along with historical evidence and current events that all can be pointed at Emmanuel Macron of France as the future-revealed Antichrist. Now you may ask, could it still be someone else and not Macron? Well, as I've mentioned several times, there are over 50 Biblical passages of characteristics, and if only one doesn't match, that's enough to disqualify a candidate. The problem is if the final seven years started tomorrow, someone today would have had to meet all the bullet points we covered. Unless I've missed someone through my extensive research, the only one that meets the Biblical criteria right now on this planet is Emmanuel Macron. Yes, about half the attributes are still yet to be fulfilled however those attributes can only be fulfilled during the final seven-year period. So one would think if a person has, with astronomical odds, already met half of the required attributes prior to the final seven years. That person will likely be the person to continue fulfilling them during the final seven years. Who else would qualify? No one.

If you are still skeptical and all I have done is raise your attention towards Emmanuel Macron as a person of interest to watch closely going forward, then I consider that an accomplishment and well worth the effort of taking the risk of writing this book.

APEC Summit November 18, 2022

ANTICHRIST UNMASKED

FULL ARMOR OF GOD

Some would say, I know times are evil and we seem to be drawing closer to the rapture of the Church, but what difference does it really make if we know now who the Antichrist is? What purpose does this serve? Most who would ask these questions believe Christians will not be here to see the Antichrist. They say we will be raptured before the tribulation begins because Christians aren't appointed to God's wrath. This traditional eschatology being taught to the Church is dangerous and reckless. It's an ear-tickling theology that absolutely is unbiblical in every instance. We have already discussed in this book that the final seven years are Biblically not the wrath of God. Only the seven bowls are filled with the wrath of God. Those do not occur until the very end, and we, as Christians, will not suffer God's wrath due to these bowls. Often ignored, we also learned that *2 Thessalonians 2:3* plainly states that two pre-requisites must happen before the rapture, one being that the "man of sin" must be revealed first. We also have learned that Antichrist will not be globally revealed until the halfway point of the final seven years.

In this book's introduction, I gave a short answer to both of these questions that most pre-tribulation rapture proponents ask. The Bible gives us so much information about the Antichrist for us to recognize and **expose** him. When Antichrist is revealed, global spiritual warfare will be at a level never seen before in history or ever will be seen again in the future. The mandate for the Church during this time will be to continue the Great Commission leading those away from Antichrist and to the only truth; Jesus Christ. This is why it makes a difference in knowing who Antichrist is and our purpose by exposing him.

As the last generation of Saints on this planet that will be here for this final spiritual battle, we must be prepared for a kind of war we have never encountered. This war will be a spiritual battle that will use weapons by our enemy in the physical realm. 2,000 years ago, Jesus came to earth in the physical realm to fight and win a spiritual battle on our behalf. Jesus lived a perfect life, died, was buried, and rose again on the third day as the victory over sin for anyone who believes in Him as their savior. We are getting ready to encounter where the unseen spiritual battle that has been happening all around us is getting ready to show itself in our physical realm again. This time it will be Satan incarnate as Antichrist. Evil is becoming more brazen and in your face today than I have ever seen. This is the spirit of the Antichrist. I don't think I'm alone in saying that ever since 2020, everything has seemed to shift suddenly into a darker direction than we were in before 2020. I'm not trying to put fear into anyone. As a matter of fact, the sooner we as Christians can get over any fear we may carry, then that will be when God can use us to our fullest potential.

7For God has not given us a spirit of fear, but of power and of love and of a sound mind. 2 Timothy 1:7 NKJV

Knowing and applying Bible prophecy will allow God's people to endure to the end. On the flip side, the Bible also states, *"for the lack of knowledge my people perish Hosea 4:6."* The popular pre-tribulation rapture theory is not preparing Christians at all. I have no anger toward my fellow Brothers in Christ who lead and preach the gospel. My indignation is toward Satan and the delusion he has created for the Church heading into the last days. This is one of the primary reasons I've written the few books I have written. I'm trying to help connect clear dots concerning Bible prophecy to wake up and better equip the Saints, Pastors, and Leaders of the faith. A proper understanding *(hear)* of Bible prophecy will be a *"blessing"* for those during the final seven years. Think about it; if you already know what will happen before it happens, then this knowledge will give you the advantage and ability to physically prepare for specific events and navigate them. God will be able to use you on the other side of some of these events, *i.e.*, continue to spread the gospel.

*3**Blessed** is he who **reads** and those who **hear** the words of this prophecy, and keep those things which are written in it; for the time is near. Revelation 1:3 NKJV*

For example, we know that the final seven years begin with the confirmation of the covenant of *Daniel 9:27*. This event will launch the final seven years until Jesus returns for His Church! If you haven't already, when you see this event happen, it will probably be a good time to get yourself physically prepared with food, etc. Why? Because the Bible says when they say peace and safety, then sudden destruction will follow *1 Thessalonians 5:3*. This destruction will more than likely be through a world war, as mentioned in *Revelation chapter 9* and *Ezekiel chapters 38-39*. Some would say you are just a

crazy prepper without faith. When you are prepared for something that you know without a doubt will be happening soon, you would be foolish not to prepare for it. There are several examples of God's people preparing physically for things God told them were coming. For instance, Joseph stockpiled food for Egypt because he knew a seven-year drought was coming, etc.

The talk of Peace and War is at a head-on collision course with one another as I'm writing currently. If you think the supply chain is not great now, wait and see what it's like after a world war that the Bible states will eliminate 1/3 of humanity. After this war, you will need to begin to prepare at least two more times physically. Right before the Abomination of desolation and before the "mark of the beast" is administered during the seventh year. Christians will not be participating in an economy that utilizes a mark that will be placed on your right hand or forehead. I don't expect this new way of living to get off its feet well before God starts dismantling it. The first bowl of God's wrath is directed toward those that have taken this mark. The Bible says that they break out in very smelly and gruesome sores all over their bodies. As Christians, the ministry of the gospel will be over. We will be waiting on God to accomplish his will through these bowls of wrath upon the world. After these bowls, Jesus will be coming to get us. Just like the Jews were set free after the ten plagues God placed on Egypt. They were protected throughout the administering of the plagues; we, too, are sealed and will be protected through these bowl events. Some have calculated that the ten plagues of Egypt took approximately 30 days to complete. When we see the mark of the beast administered, we will know that our redemption is only days away; however, it will be a time to physically hunker down and get spiritually ready. This may be the extra 75 days of time accounted for that the book of Daniel mentions.

So I've just given you one tangible example of how knowing Bible prophecy will be beneficial in preparing you physically to navigate the times ahead. This chapter's primary point is to "spiritually" prepare you for a particular battle on the horizon. Satan will be making war with the Saints. We are the last generation of Saints the book of Revelation is referencing. For the past couple of years, God has been giving us loud warnings of things that are soon to come into fruition. These warnings should not be ignored while we get our houses in order and prepared.

This soon-to-be spiritual battle that's about to merge into our physical realm is not hyperbole. For example, you will see the Antichrist and False Prophet exhibiting supernatural wonders to draw people to themselves; *Revelation 13:13-14*. The two witnesses God sends represent the spiritual into our physical; they will be on our side; *Revelation ch 11*. The fallen angels who are followers of Satan will be banished to earth, unable to go back and forth into the heavenly realms. This evil spiritual presence here now will be manifested in our physical realm to be seen, and Satan will know his time is short.

*7It was granted to him to **make war with the Saints and to overcome them**. And authority was given him over every tribe, tongue, and nation. 8All who dwell on the earth will worship him, whose names have not been written in the Book of Life of the Lamb slain from the foundation of the world. Revelation 13:7-8 NKJV*

25He shall speak pompous words against the Most High,
***Shall persecute the Saints** of the Most High,*
And shall intend to change times and law.
*Then **the Saints shall be given into his hand***
*For **a time and times and half a time**. Daniel 7:25 NKJV*

ANTICHRIST UNMASKED

This is not an easy chapter; however, ignoring these difficult passages is not an option. Those who have a proper understanding of the times we live in and are about to encounter will be better equipped and prepared for battle. Yes, it will be a battle! Again, the Bible states Satan will make war with the Saints. We know from Daniel that the battle against the Saints will begin at the 3 1/2-year point. Time, times, and half a time signify 3 1/2 years. The term *"be given into his hand"* means we will be under a global dictator whose target will be the Jews and Christians. Jews and Christians have been persecuted throughout history but will pale in comparison to the final 3 1/2 years called the Great Tribulation Mathew 24:21.

The fact that Satan will have to make war with the Saints is a sign we will be a formable opponent against him.

*32Those who do wickedly against the covenant he shall corrupt with flattery; but **the people who know their God shall be strong, and carry out great exploits**. 33And those of the people who understand shall instruct many…*
Daniel 11:32-33 NKJV

This passage in Daniel is what is happening during the final 3 1/2 years after the confirmation of the covenant. Notice that it also states that *"the people who understand shall instruct many."* I pray you will be one of those people. This implies there will be many Christians during this time confused, having to be instructed by those who have a clear understanding of Bible prophecy in order to navigate correctly. This confusion is what gives Antichrist an advantage during this time. Again, the popular pre-tribulation left behind crowd is not preparing the Church for what's coming; otherwise, there wouldn't be a need to instruct so many Christians during the time Daniel is speaking about.

As we see events drawing us closer to the final seven years, we need to expose evil now and inform and warn the Church. We can do this while still reaching those with the Gospel of Christ.

During the final seven years, we will have a mandate, which will be the mandate we have had for the past 2,000 years. The mandate will be to reach as many people to Christ as possible before the rapture. The difference, especially during the final 3 1/2 years, is that spiritual warfare will be at a level this world has never seen before. God, through his word, gives us some advice for spiritual battles. It is to put on the FULL ARMOR OF GOD.

*10Finally, my brethren, be strong in the Lord and in the power of His might. 11**Put on the whole armor of God**, that you may be able **to stand against the wiles of the devil**. 12For we do not wrestle against flesh and blood, but against principalities, against powers, against the rulers of the darkness of this age, against spiritual hosts of wickedness in the heavenly places. 13Therefore **take up***

the whole armor of God, that you may be able to withstand in the evil day, and having done all, to stand. 14Stand therefore, having girded your waist with truth, having put on the breastplate of righteousness, 15and having shod your feet with the preparation of the gospel of peace; 16above all, taking the shield of faith with which you will be able to quench all the fiery darts of the wicked one. 17And take the helmet of salvation, and the sword of the Spirit, which is the word of God; 18praying always with all prayer and supplication in the Spirit, being watchful to this end with all perseverance and supplication for all the Saints— 19and for me, that utterance may be given to me, that I may open my mouth boldly to make known the mystery of the gospel, 20for which I am an ambassador in chains; that in it I may speak boldly, as I ought to speak.
Ephesians 6:10-20 NKJV

God offers you the same armor that he protects himself with. In the book of Isaiah, we are told, *"He put on righteousness as a breastplate And a helmet of salvation on His head..."* **(Isaiah 59:17)**

While every day has its share of evil, not every day is the "evil day" *vs. 13*. This entire passage applies to the everyday life as a Christian to be fearless, strong, and courageous as we are living our lives as a witness for Jesus in this wicked dark world. Paul is also making it clear that there will be a specific time when evil will have its fulfillment. *"In the evil day"* is in direct reference to the last days when Antichrist is given authority to rule, the Great Tribulation. Paul isn't speaking to anyone left behind. He is speaking to the last generation of Saints living *"In the evil day."* That is you and me.

We are told to take up the whole armor of God. This implies there is a choice on your part to put the armor on. Sometimes in life, we choose to utilize certain pieces of armor while leaving other pieces aside. By being partially dressed for battle, you are leaving yourself vulnerable. Paul, with a sense of urgency, tells us more than once to put on the whole armor of God before he even begins to explain each piece of armor.

Belt of Truth
Wearing the belt of Truth means safeguarding yourself with the Truth of Jesus. Jesus is the embodiment of Truth. Jesus, in *John 14:6*, proclaimed himself as the Truth. We are living in a time of deception like never before. The first thing Jesus warns us about during the last days is, *"Take heed that no one deceives you" Matthew 24:4*. When Pilate confronted Jesus just before his crucifixion, Jesus told Pilate why he came to earth. His answer was, *"I should bear witness to the Truth."* Jesus qualifies the fact that his followers are of the Truth. This comment regarding his followers being the Truth refers back to himself.

*37Pilate therefore said to Him, "Are You a king then?" Jesus answered, "You say rightly that I am a king. For this cause I was born, and for this cause **I have come into the world, that I should bear witness to the truth.** Everyone who is of the truth hears My voice." John 18:37 NKJV*

We, as Christians, are to bear witness to the Truth to the whole world in this time of darkness and confusion. We are vessels of Truth because of our relationship with Jesus. Jesus is the Truth which means everything, and anyone else proclaiming to be the Truth is a lie. We should point people to the person who embodies complete Truth, Jesus.

Breastplate of Righteousness

We are to claim for ourselves the righteousness before God that only comes from Christ. When you give your life to Jesus, you are covered in Christ's blood, which declares you are blameless before God, and His righteousness allows you to grow in your obedience as the Holy Spirit changes you. We need to focus on obeying God's will and saying no to sin as we are actively living out the righteousness we have through our relationship with Jesus.

By placing on the breastplate of righteousness during these final days, we are being purified, made white, and refined as the bride of Christ (Church) preparing herself for the bridegroom (Jesus). The final seven years are more so to prepare the Church to meet Jesus as a "spiritually" beautiful bride than it is for the final wrath that will be poured out immediately after we depart from this world.

10Many shall be purified, made white, and refined, but the wicked shall do wickedly; and none of the wicked shall understand, but the wise shall understand. Daniel 12:10

Shoes of the Gospel

15and having shod your feet with the preparation of the gospel of peace

During times of uncertainty like we are living in today. The global leaders and the world's solutions are not who people need to put their hope in. Often governments create chaos to afterward swoop in as having the answers to the problems they just created. This is deception so that you will put your trust in the government. The Antichrist will also be using such schemes.

*25And **through his policy** also he shall **cause craft to prosper** in his hand; and he shall magnify himself in his heart, and **by peace shall destroy many**: Daniel 8:25 KJV*

As we are living in days that are becoming darker, we need to be fully prepared to walk through these troubled times ahead with the gospel of peace to all that come across our path, hurting and looking for answers. Family members, people at work, and whoever we may encounter as we go about life need to know Jesus is our only solution. We should also stand firm in our shoes of the gospel without fear of those that intend harm against us because we bear the light of Jesus.

*"And **do not be afraid** of their threats, nor be troubled." 15But sanctify the Lord God in your hearts, and always be ready to give a defense to everyone who asks you a reason for the hope that is in you, with meekness and fear 1 Peter 3:14-15 NKJV*

Shield of Faith
We are told to take up the shield of faith as we battle. What is faith?

1Now faith is the substance of things hoped for, the evidence of things not seen. Hebrews 11:1 NKJV

As you continue to live your life out for Jesus during these last days, you can be sure that this will not go unrecognized by Satan. We are quickly approaching the final seven years, and during the last half of the seven-year period, he will make war against the Saints. I believe it's because we will be making such an impact against his plans that he will know his time is running out. In a panic, Antichrist will carry out ruthless behavior as a last-ditch effort of world domination to eliminate the presence of any

Christians. The shield of faith is one of the strongest weapons against Satan's attacks.

*"16above all, taking the **shield of faith** with which you will be able to quench all the fiery darts of the wicked one."*

Satan will try to cast lies and accusations against you in order to diminish your spiritual will to carry on. We see this already today. Satan's "fiery darts" can come in many forms, including physical. Our "faith" during these times serves our purpose as a shield against anything Satan tries to use. Every day that goes by is a day closer to the soon coming of our lord and savior. If you are living to be utilized by God during the final seven years, Bible prophecy can affirm and strengthen your faith. Think about it after waiting for nearly 2,000 years, when the final seven years begin, we will be only seven years from the rapture of the Church! That final seventh trumpet will sound, and you will see Jesus face to face! There will be nothing Satan can do to thwart my faith once the final seven years begin!

*16For the Lord Himself will descend from heaven with a shout, with the voice of an archangel, and with the trumpet of God. And the dead in Christ will rise first. 17Then we who are alive and remain shall be caught up together with them in the clouds to meet the Lord in the air. And thus we shall always be with the Lord. **18Therefore comfort one another with these words.** 1 Thessalonians 4:16-18 NKJV*

Helmet of Salvation
The absolute assurance of salvation can give you the confidence to enter the battle and, if necessary, take some blows.

Your salvation is the most amazing gift Jesus could ever give you. Meditating on salvation that can never be lost is empowering over any thoughts of fear that may creep into your mind.

*39This is the will of the Father who sent Me, that of all He has given Me **I should lose nothing**, but should raise it up at the **last day**. 40And this is the will of Him who sent Me, that **everyone who sees the Son and believes in Him** may have **everlasting life**; and I will raise him up at the **last day**." John 6:39-40 NKJV*

*13In Him you also trusted, after you heard the word of truth, the gospel of your salvation; in whom also, having believed, you were **sealed with the Holy Spirit of <u>promise</u>**, 14who is the **<u>guarantee of our inheritance</u> until the redemption of the purchased possession,** to the praise of His glory. Ephesians 1:13-14 NKJV*

If you have given your life to Jesus, your body becomes the temple of the living Holy Spirit, who will guide and protect you and seals you until the day of redemption (rapture); therefore, you can never lose your salvation.

Before putting on any piece of the Armor of God, you must first be in a relationship with Jesus, who enables you to be appropriately suited up for battle. Do you have the Helmet of Salvation? I'm not asking if you know who Jesus is but rather do you have a relationship with Jesus? There is a difference. Satan himself knows Jesus, but his end destination is the bottomless pit. If you are unsure if you have a relationship with Jesus and want this vital piece of armor, "The Helmet of Salvation," the Bible tells us how we can be saved.

*9that if **you confess** with your mouth the **Lord Jesus** and **believe** in your heart that **God has raised Him from the dead, <u>you will be saved.</u>***
*10For with the **heart one believes** unto righteousness, and with the **mouth confession is made unto salvation.** 11For the Scripture says, "**Whoever believes** on Him will not be put to shame." 12**For there is no distinction between Jew***

and Greek, for the same Lord over all is rich to all who call upon Him. 13For "whoever calls on the name of the Lord shall be saved." Roman 10:9-13 NKJV

You could pray something like this in your own words straight from your heart:

Lord Jesus, I know I'm a sinner, and I ask for forgiveness of my sins. I believe you died on the cross and rose on the third day so I could receive your forgiveness and eternal life. I ask that you come into my life and be my Lord and Savior. I give you control over my life and ask that you help me to live for you from this day forward. Amen.

If you have just given your life to Jesus, your name is written in the Lambs' book of Life, and His Holy Spirit has sealed you for the day of redemption. Jesus will be coming back for you! Congratulations! You just received your first piece of armor, the Helmet of Salvation.

Your Purpose in life is simple; don't live by fear; instead, go out as the victorious Christian you are and be the light of Christ in this dark world for everyone around you to see, for Jesus Is coming soon!

*14"**You are the light of the world**. A city that is set on a hill cannot be hidden. 15Nor do they light a lamp and put it under a basket, but on a lampstand, and it gives light to all who are in the house. 16**Let your light so shine before men**, that they may see your good works and glorify your Father in heaven. Matthew 5:14-16 NKJV*

Find yourself a Bible-believing church for community. Though baptism is not a requirement for salvation, it does symbolize outwardly, much like a wedding band does, that you now have a relationship with Jesus; your baptism is a great witness for those that are lost.

The Sword of the Spirit

The sword of the spirit is the word of God, the Bible. The sword is a weapon meant to be used on the offensive. Jesus used scripture against Satan during His 40 days in the wilderness. When we feel we may be under attack, we can use scripture to cut through any attack by the enemy. The Bible exposes one's heart and intent. In a day of such deception and flat-out lies, using scripture leaves anyone trying to perpetrate evil against you without any excuse.

*12For the **word of God** is living and powerful, and **sharper than any two-edged sword**, piercing even to the division of soul and spirit, and of joints and marrow, and is a discerner of the thoughts and intents of the heart. 13And there is no creature hidden from His sight, but all things are naked and open to the eyes of Him to whom we must give account. Hebrews 4:12-13 NKJV*

Paul ends by telling us to pray always in the Spirit. The prayer of the righteous is strong and effective. The power of prayer gives every Christian access to the throne of God through his Holy Spirit. God wants us to abide in Him through our Bible and prayer life, and we can request anything good from Him.

16Confess your trespasses to one another, and pray for one another, that you may be healed. The effective, fervent prayer of a righteous man avails much. James 5:16 NKJV

By properly suiting up for battle, we can have the confidence to proclaim the Gospel of Jesus to the world boldly. Our primary battle is not against flesh and blood but against principalities and evil powers of the rulers of darkness. When wearing the full armor of God, we are lending ourselves to be used by God in mighty ways at a time when we need more Christians to confront the evil of our day boldly while at the same time reaching the world to Jesus.

*11And have no fellowship with the unfruitful works of darkness, but rather **expose them**. 12For it is **shameful** even to speak of those things which are done by them **in secret**. 13<u>But all things that are exposed are made manifest by the light, for whatever makes manifest is light.</u> 14Therefore He says:*

*"**Awake**, you who sleep,*
***Arise** from the dead,*
*And Christ will give you **light**." Ephesians 5:11-14 NKJV*

You may also want to take a look at these books.

ANTICHRIST UNMASKED

Final Word From The Author

God chose you to live through this Biblically prophetic time in history for his glory! He wouldn't have allowed you to be born during these times that will soon lead to his return if he didn't think you were capable of shining for him. He sees greatness in you! He sees greatness in the remnant of his Church!

C. S. DeCaro

Want to receive Bible Prophecy Updates? Send an e-mail with your **NAME** and the words **"PLEASE SUBSCRIBE"** in the subject line to: **TheEndTimeIsNow@icloud.com**

I don't use social media and need some help spreading the word. One way is to leave a positive star rating on Amazon and the second is to copy and paste a link of this book to your social media pages, it would go a long way in helping send out a warning flare to those in your realm of reach. God Bless.

Scan, copy & paste from browser:

Bibliography

(Scannable Resources)

New King James Version Bible, NKJV

King James Version Bible, KJV

New American Standard Bible, NASB

biblegateway.com (Used for interactive links)

FREE BIBLE APP ——————————————————

Blue Letter Bible (Used for original Greek Strong's concordance, It's FREE)

britannica.com/place/Vatican-City ———

news.tfionline.com/big-brother-in-india-requires-fingerprint-scans

 nypost.com/2019/07/14/swedish-people-are-getting-chip-implants-to-replace-cash-credit-cards

 marketwatch.com/states-are-cracking-down-on-companies-microchipping-their-employees 2020-02-03

 usgoldbureau.com/news/new-york-fed-begins-12-week-cbdc-settlement-pilot-test

 jpost.pressreader.com/article/Israeli Palistinian peace talks in Moscow

 meaningofthename.com

 chimpanzee's DNA and humans "Genesis apologetics"

 britannica.com/biography/Emmanuel Macron

younggloballeaders.org/community

geopolitics.co/2022/02/22/world-economic-forums-young-global-leaders-revealed

technocracy.news/world-economic-forums-young-global-leaders-revealed

cnn.com/2017/05/07/europe/macron-le-pen-french-election-results

breitbart.com/europe/2017/07/04/macron-announces-govern-like-jupiter-roman-king-gods

townandcountrymag.com/society/politics/emmanuel-macron-prince

ANTICHRIST UNMASKED

 politico.eu/article/emmanuel-macrons-eu-defense-army-coalition-of-the-willing-military-cooperation

 thoughtco.com/profile-of-the-roman-god-jupiter-119328

 bible-history.com/sketches/jupiter-the-chief-god-of-rome

 bbc.com/news/world-europe-"Complex Thinker"Macron

 cruxnow.com/vatican/2018/06/is-french-leaders-pope-visit-a-homecoming-for-churchs-eldest-daughter

 riviera-buzz.com/features/news/item/french-president-honorary-canon-of-archbasilica-of-st-john-lateran.

lifesitenews.com/news/pro-abortion-french-president-macron-accepts-papal-honor-in-rome

news.yahoo.com/bodyguard-scandal-exposes-limits-macrons-jupiterian-style

compellingtruth.org/Antiochus-Epiphanes

jewishencyclopedia.com/articles/ptolemy-macron

albawaba.com/news/macron-plants-cedar-tree-lebanon-underlines-special-relationship-france

ejpress.org/french-president-macron-on-israels-independence-day-you-know-my-deep-attachment-to-israel

thoughtco.com/rulers-of-france-from 840-present

ANTICHRIST UNMASKED

 agbi.com/analysis/sheikh-mohamed-france-emmanuel-macron

 thenationalnews.com/world/2022/07/28/saudi-arabias-crown-prince-mohammed-bin-salman-meets-emmanuel-macron-in-paris

 voanews.com/a/israel-s-lapid-meets-macron-in-paris-on-first-trip-as-pm

 timesofisrael.com/palestinian-authority-president-abbas-to-meet-frances-macron-in-paris

 jta.org/2022/09/22/israel/yair-lapid-recommits-israel-to-the-two-state-solution-in-un-speech

 timesofisrael.com/macron-phones-netanyahu-to-congratulate-him-on-election-win

 thedefensepost.com/2022/11/09/france-uk-defense-summit

VIDEOS

Yuval Noah Harari

Prince/King Charles

Prime M. Yair Lapid
U.N.

Emmanuel Macron
Devil Horns

Emmanuel Macron
APEC Nov. 2022

Macron Victory Rally
E.U. anthem

Macron's visit with
Pope

Grocery Stores
Prep for Beast System

I want to give a special thanks to my daughter, who helped with QR technology integration into the paperback version. With my daughter's help, the book was brought to the next level.

Made in the USA
Coppell, TX
10 July 2025

51693309R10090